The Comprehensive Guide

To

Passing the Indiana Real Estate Sales Exam

Real Estate Review

Types of Property

There are two main types of property that are discussed in real estate. They are *real* property and *personal* property. Real property mainly refers to the land and things or items that are permanently attached to it, such as plant life, ground minerals, and even buildings such as houses or offices. Things that grow on the property, such as trees, flowers and various other plants are considered part of the real property and are generally included with the land as a whole. Any fixture that causes damage to the property when it is moved is considered a real piece of property. When a person owns real property, they have more rights to its surrounding areas such as surface rights or air rights.

There are two types of personal property: tangibles and intangible. Tangible personal property refers to property that is more tangible and moveable, such as furniture, swing sets, or mobile fixtures. Although plant life is generally seen as real property, it can be classified as personal property if it is superficially planted and can be moved when the property is sold. Personal property does not generally include many rights to the land and subpart rights. Intangible personal property includes intellectual property such as patents.

Sometimes, personal property can become real property if it later becomes a permanent fixture of the land. For instance, if a house is built on a secure and sturdy foundation and cannot later be moved from the property, it has become part of the real property. However, a home such as an RV or mobile home can be moved from the property at any time, so it remains a piece of personal property.

Land Characteristics

There are many characteristics to describe land and land function. The main two that are considered are the physical characteristics and the economic characteristics.

Physical characteristics of land:

- **Immobility** – Land cannot be moved in its entirety, therefore it is considered immobile. Although pieces can be removed or replaced, the original part of the land still remains and will continue to grow.

- **Indestructibility** – Although land can be damaged by storms or disasters, it cannot be ultimately destroyed because it continues to change, adjust and develop over time. This is one of the main reasons land is considered such a valuable asset and investment.

- **Non-homogeneity** – Simply states that no two pieces of land are alike. Note the different features and location of items on each parcel of land and how they differ from the whole 'package'.

Economic characteristics of land:

- **Scarcity** – In many areas, land itself is considered a rarity, and owning a parcel of land can seem even more outrageous. When land is scarce and there is little to own, it not only drives up the face price, but it will also add value as an investment over time.

- **Improvements** – In many cases, minor improvements, such as decorative touches or adding a bathroom will not affect the economic value on the home, and may even work against the owner. However, structural upgrades, such as replacing the roof or replacing a broken wall, can add value to the home since they are improving the initial foundation of it. Many homeowners confuse these two and can make their house not as economic as they'd like.

- **Permanence** – Also known as 'fixity', permanence refers to the lasting potential of the land or property. Owners want to know that their property will be long term in nature and that what they have built on or created and cannot easily be moved or destroyed.

- **Situs** – Situs is the knowledge that some owners prefer specific locations, which can drive the value of the property up or down. Since the preferences of owners and buyers are always changing, this can be hard to determine at one point in time.

Encumbrances

An encumbrance is generally defined as a claim or lien on a parcel of real property. If a property has some sort of encumbrance attached to its title, it can be difficult to determine the proper owner and who has the rights to the property. Specific types of encumbrances include:

- **Encroachment** – A situation in which a structure or fixture is built on another person's property or land, and 'encroaches' on their area. This often happens due to incorrect surveying or incorrect marked boundary lines.

- **Easement** – A certain right to use the real property of another owner, such as paying rent for a building on their land or being allowed access to a privately owned lake. While the individual rights of the easement can vary, the easement is still considered a property right and is treated as such in courts of law.

    - **Easement Appurtenant** – Typically benefits the land and is transferred automatically if the property is transferred to another party – "runs with the land".

    - **Easement in Gross** – Typically benefits the individual or legal party and can be used for personal or commercial use. While this type of easement is not inherited or assignable, it can be transferred for business purposes.

- **Liens** – The official definition is "is a form of security granted over an item of property to secure the payment of a debt or obligation". Many liens require some form of documentation and specific guidelines that need to be followed.

    - **Mechanic's lien** – a lien that exists for real and personal property and initiated by those who have supplied labor or materials to improve the property (carpenters, landscapers).

    - **Material Man's lien** – similar to a mechanic's lien, but applies more to the actual person or company who supplies the actual materials being used.

- **Foreclosure** – a legal process in which the lender tries to recover the balance of a loan after payments have stopped, by selling the asset used as collateral for the loan. This is a very common term/practice with houses and property.

- **Judgment** – A type of lien that is meant to secure payment or property that was awarded in some kind of judgment or settlement.

    - **Writ of attachment** – a court order to seize an asset.

    - **Writ of execution** – written in order to force a judgment made against an asset, usually to collect an asset that has been ordered to be turned over.

- **Tax liens** – A type of lien obtained on the property, including all land rights, imposed by the government's taxing authority – typically used for payment of federal taxes.

- **Property tax lien** – a lien to seize assets on a property or set of properties.
- **Federal tax lien** – a lien to seize federal taxes that have not been paid.
- **State tax lien** – a lien to seize state taxes that have not yet been paid.

Liens can be considered voluntary or involuntary in different cases. A homeowner may choose to enter a lien he takes out a second mortgage on his home. However, the lien may not be voluntary if the government obtains a lien to the property in order to secure payment for back taxes and fees.

One common example of an involuntary lien is when a contractor is hired for work on the property, but when the owner doesn't pay for the job, the contractor can put a lien on the property to secure his/her payment. Since the general statute of limitations is four years for the contractor to pursue his claim, he can claim a lien long after the work is done. If this happens, the property owner will need to hire a lawyer to either reach a settlement or fight the claim in a court of law.

Ownership Types

When referring to ownership titles, it is important to remind the seller of the property that is it his responsibility to convey the marketable title to the public. The seller must be aware of instances that can make the property 'unmarketable', such as encumbrances, zoning restrictions, or outstanding interests. If the seller cannot produce a clear deed to the property, the buyer will be unaware of the full ownership.

- **Title search** – a process designed to determine if a seller of property has saleable interest, any restrictions or allowance for a property or any liens/foreclosures.
- **Chain of title** – a 'chain' of transfers of a title to a property. It usually involves investigating the line of previous owners up to the current owner.
- **Grantee index** – an alphabetic list of purchasers of the property.
- **Grantor index** – an alphabetical list of sellers of the property.

Terms to remember:

- **Estate in severalty** – a form of ownership in which the tenant owns the property without being joined in interest with another party.

- **Tenancy in common** – a form of ownership in which two parties possess the property simultaneously, created by a deed, final will or court order.

- **Joint Tenancy** – a form of ownership in which two parties own an undivided interest in the property. With joint tenancy, the right of survivorship is applicable. This means that a co-owner cannot designate a new owner to take over his interest when he dies. Instead, the surviving co-owner will automatically take over the decedent's interest.
  - **Unity of time** – interest acquired by both tenants at the same time.
  - **Unity of title** – interests held by co-owners from the same property.
  - **Unity of interest** – both tenants have the same interest in the same property.
  - **Unity of possession** – both tenants have the same right to the property.

- **Community property** – a form of ownership commonly defined as property owned by spouses – can also be owner through a partnership established by law.

- **Partnerships** – a property contract in which two people enter ownership equally together, each sharing in profits and losses from the property. A joint venture is similar to a partnership, usually involves a 'project' and is normally set for a limited amount of time.
  - **General partnership** – basic form of partnership; an association of people or unincorporated company that creates an agreement formed by two or more people and all parties are responsible for action, debts, and liability that occurs on the property.
  - **Limited partnership** – a partnership in which only one person is required to be a general partner, but both parties share in profits, debts and liability from the property.

- **Corporations** – a legal entity that has been incorporated and holds equal rights and liability for the property through a charter.

- **Fee simple estate** – a form of common law ownership; very popular in common law countries but still has restrictions by the government, such as taxation, police power and liability.

Property Descriptions

There are many different types of property and property deeds. Each one gives different characteristics to the property in question and can change the whole context in which someone views it.

- **Metes and bounds** – a method of describing real property that uses geography and land features with direction and distances to define and describe the boundaries of the land.

- **Rectangular survey system** – traditional method of surveying property and measures factors such as the precise length of line run, natural materials (flora/fauna), surface and land soil.

- **Government or US public land system** – Most commonly used method to survey and spatially identify land or property parcels before designating ownership, whether for sale or transfer.

- **Congressional townships** – a survey method that refers to a square unit of land, that is usually six miles on each side. Each 36 square mile township is divided into 36 one-square mile sections that can be further subdivided for sale.

- **Principal meridians** – method that uses a principal meridian line used for survey control in a large region, which divides townships between north/south/east/west. The meridian meets its corresponding initial point for the land survey.

- **Recorded plat** – also known as the lot and block survey system; this system is used for lots in a variety of areas (i.e. heavily populated metropolitan, suburban, and exurbs). Especially used to plot large areas of a property into smaller lots and land areas.

- Example plat map

Source: http://en.wikipedia.org/wiki/Lot_and_Block_survey_system

- **Assessor's parcel number** – also known as an appraisal's account number; a number assigned to parcels of property by the area's jurisdiction for identification and record-keeping. This APN is unique within the particular jurisdiction, and may conform to certain formatting standards that hold identifying information, such as the property type or location within the plat map.

Rights of Government in Land

The government can often draw a fine line as to where they have rights to land and where they don't. However, the U.S. government has the right to take private property for public use through the power of eminent [domain](#) and expropriation or taking power.

Escheatment is the transfer of one's property who doesn't have heirs when he/she dies. This process helps ensure that the property is not left unattended and appoints someone accountable for it, so as not to leave it in 'limbo'. Escheatments are commonly done when the owner of the estate passes away or loses ownership, although it can occur voluntarily between willing parties.

Property taxes are required on all land owned/financed in an area and are paid to the government. Multiple areas, or jurisdictions, can tax the same property at a time if it is being utilized in more than one area or claims more than one address. The tax is imposed by the government in which the property is located. It is made payable to the federal or state government. For property tax purposes, the government performs an appraisal of the quantity and value of each property, including real property and any improvements, and tax is assessed in proportion to that value. Appraisals are required by the government to assure that the property is being taxed appropriately.

Ad valorem taxes are taxes created specifically based on the monetary value of the property as a whole. This is the most common type of property tax and is usually created at the time of the purchase of the property, although it can be done on an annual basis as well.

Gains and Losses

A capital gain is realized when the property is sold and the sale price is more than the price that it was initially purchased for. Many jurisdictions impose a capital gains tax and require several forms of documentation to ensure accurate transactions.

Depreciation generally refers to the decrease in value over time. This can occur due to unfavored home modifications, damages, or changes in property costs and prices.

Estates

"Estate" generally refers to a person's property, entitlements or assets, but is usually applied to a large parcel of land that includes the real and personal property. It is usually defined as the houses and grounds of a very large property, including woodlands, farmlands, gardens or landscapes. Estates are generally owned by individual or joint ownership or title by contract.

- **Freehold estate** – an estate that has the exclusive right to the possession and use of the property for an indefinite amount of time.

  Fee simple absolute - the most common type of freehold estate ownership. This gives the owner a variety of rights, such as:

  -The authority to live in, rent or mortgage the property

  -The authority to sell destroy or reassign ownership of the property

  -The authority to construct buildings on the property

  -The authority to excavate minerals, gas and oil

  -The authority to refuse the use of property by others

- **Non freehold estate** – an estate similar to a lease or contract situation that holds limited rights and usage to the property and typically has a set or predetermined time period for the tenant.

- **Fee upon condition** – the fees/taxes of the property based on outside circumstances, such as home modifications, outside liens or holds on the property, or changes in the real estate market.

- **Life estate** – an estate that ends at the death of the owner and reverts to the original owner. The owner of the life estate is called the life tenant, and is designated ownership of the land for the duration of their life.

- **Pur autre vie** – "for another's life" - similar to a life estate, it states that a person's life interest will last for the life of another person's life instead of their own.

- **Remainderman** – an individual who inherits property when an estate is terminated from the former owner. This typically happens due to the death of the owner's life estate, but can also be a voluntary act.

- **Life estate in reversion** – a life estate ownership that 'reverts' back to the original owner or grantor.

If an estate wants/needs to be transferred between parties, it is usually done by one of two ways:

Deeds – deeds can be transferred from one party/person to another, usually done through the county office and completed while both parties are present; this process is usually voluntary but can be done involuntarily if ordered by a court of law.

Will/inheritance – deeds transferred after the original owner dies and designates it to another party; if a party is not assigned, the government can take control of the land and use it as they see fit (putting it up for sale or reassigning survey lines).

Governments Controls

Forms of public controls:

- Police power – government entities typically 'control' the rights to the property by creating laws or guidelines that must be followed when owning a parcel of property. Some common examples include development and zoning laws, which designate or restrict what structures or improvements can be made on the property. City codes, such as building or fire codes, often place restrictions on the occupancy of a property and can determine how a property is used or maintained.

- Eminent domain – the power to take private property for public use by a state, municipality, or private person or corporation; some common examples of property taken by eminent domain are for government buildings and facilities, highways or railroads or for public safety hazards.
    - Condemnation – the process of exercising powers of eminent domain
    - Severance damage – payment to a property owner for an inconvenience that is caused once a portion or all of the land is purchased and used under eminent domain.
    - Inverse condemnation – a situation where the government seizes the property, but fails to pay the compensation required by the 5th Amendment rights of the Constitution.

- Consequential damage – damages you can prove occurred because of the failure of one party to meet a contractual obligation; commonly referred to as a breach of contract.

- Environmental Hazards and Regulations – laws, guidelines, and regulations the government puts into place to help monitor and regulate different aspects of the country, including physical property, plant life, animals and surrounding environments.
    - The Clean Air Act – signed into law in 1970 and was aimed at controlling air pollutants produced by industrial companies. Since 1970, over 40 amendments have been added to the original law.
    - The Clean Water Act – passed in 1972 and is aimed at controlling water pollution; addresses a popular problem of water dumping by companies and individuals.
    - National Environmental Policy Act – created after the 1969 Santa Barbara oil spill; it made the entity of the property, commercial or private, responsible for ensuring the safety of the environment, including pollution or any chance of accidents.
    - Comprehensive Environmental Response, Compensation, and Liability Act (CERLA) – created in 1980, it was designed to be a 'superfund' that supplies resources to hazardous wastes sites, such as oil spills or spilled contaminants. Through CERLA, entities responsible for the spill are also responsible for the cleanup.
    - The Endangered Species Act – created in 1973 and is designed to provide protection for wildlife and flora that is at risk of becoming extinct; among many provisions, it states that animals considered endangered are not allowed to be hunted or harmed and that state government can seize any land that is needed to preserve the species.
    - The Safe Drinking Water Act – created in 1974 and was created to ensure the safety and quality of America's drinking water; it is designed to protect drinking water sources, such as rivers, lakes and reservoirs.
    - The Toxic Substances Control Act – passed in 1976 and regulates any new or existing chemical substances and their use; it requires companies to submit notifications and information regarding any new chemical created and added to the TSCA list.

- Residential Lead-Based Paint Hazard Reduction Act – passed in 1992 and aimed at reducing the number of residences that have lead-based paint, as this type of paint has been associated with many health hazards.

Forms of private controls:

Conditions – generally refers to the status of property, such as current structures and how the property is sustained. Many restrictions are attached to the condition of the property and how it will look and appear in the future.

Covenants – simply defined as a promise to uphold a requested action or use; covenant are often added to deed ownerships to restrict actions taken against the property, such as physical changes or structure formations.

Restrictions – strict prohibitions that generally 'restrict' against certain actions or behaviors; with property restrictions, the owner specifically lines out actions that cannot be done on or with the property. This can range from adding structure or modifications to restrictions on ownership and transfer of ownership.

Restrictive covenants and deed restrictions are one method that private land owners use to control the property, even after they have passed ownership to another person or party. These regulations are designed to impose rules that the owner may want to place on the property to future owners regarding new buildings, structures, or use of the land. The restrictions the owner wants to set forth are usually plainly laid out in the deed itself or in an additional covenant and are normally binding to all future owners. One common example is owners of land that restrict any use of commercial building or structures, such as condominiums or apartment buildings.

A homeowner's association (HA) is a corporation or private party formed by a real estate developer and is designed to market, manage or sell homes in a specific subdivision area. These associations are popular in metropolitan areas that group their homes in suburban divisions. Many HAs are managed by the residents that live in the division, although there are higher 'board members' that govern any final rulings or decisions. This is a form of private control because individuals that live in these divisions are often restricted on what they can do with their property, such as modifications, building add-ons or even minor home improvements.

Water Rights

Although water rights vary by state, there are two that are common nationwide. These are riparian rights and littoral rights.

- **Riparian rights** – When dealing with a navigable body of water, the property owner's boundary will reach to the water's accretion line. With a non-navigable body of water, the property owner's boundary will stop at the water's centerpoint.

- **Littoral rights** – Take into consideration the rights of a property owner whose property shares a border with a non-flowing body of water like a lake or ocean.

  Some terms to keep in mind with water rights:

  - Accretion – Natural deposit of soil that results in the steady increase in land
  - Avulsion – When water abruptly changes its course sudden, the rapid decrease in land that results
  - Erosion – When water, wind and other natural elements cause a steady decrease in land
  - Reliction – When the retreat of water causes a steady increase in land
  - Alluvion – When water shifts soil from where it is to another person's land
  - Accession – Attaining land due to the soil deposited by natural elements

Individual states issue water permits for the purpose of allotting scarce water resources, this is especially necessary in states in the west.

Other nationally recognized water rights:

- **Natural flow doctrine** – This doctrine says that if a riparian owner's use of the water causes the water to diminish in the amount, quality, or pace, it can be stopped. All riparian owners have the right to have access to the water in its natural state.

- **Doctrine of reasonable use** – As its name states, each riparian owner is entitled to reasonable use of the water. In other words, unless one owner's use severely inhibits another owner's use, it cannot be stopped. "Reasonable use" can be determined by assessing changes to water quantity, quality, velocity, pollution issues, among other things.

- **Doctrine of prior appropriation** - Refers to the water rights that are not linked to landownership. They can be sold and mortgaged in the same way other property can.

- **Doctrine of beneficial use** – States that the first users of the water are priority, but they must use the water in a beneficial manner, within a reasonable timeframe.

- **Doctrine of correlative rights** – Imposes a limit on landowners regarding their share of the water. Generally, this limit is based on the share of land owned by each.

Property Conditions

Property Condition Disclosure Forms

Usually before signing a purchase agreement, but at least before closing, salespersons/brokers are required to provide potential buyers with a document that explains the condition of the property they're looking to buy. If the proper disclosures (varies per state) have not been made, the purchase contract may become unenforceable. It is also important that rather than salespersons/brokers giving their own description of the property condition, they should encourage the potential buyers to have an inspection done.

The need for inspection

There are many instances where having an inspection done would be warranted, although not carried out. For the real estate purchaser, it is advisable that a thorough, professional inspection is done before agreeing to purchase the property. Not doing so could result in costly repairs down the line for the buyer, or even legal action against the real estate company.

Property Value

Why an Appraisal?

The first step to performing an appraisal is finding out why the appraisal should be done. Here are the more common reasons:

- condemnation: In cases where the government uses eminent domain to acquire property, the owner must be compensated fair market value.

- assessed value: In order to determine the property taxes that must be paid on the property.

- insurance reasons: So the insurance company can establish the most it will pay for a loss.

- estate settlement: In order to verify the value of a deceased individual's estate.

- sales value for owner: To determine how much the property should be sold for.

- loan value: To establish the maximum loan amount that can be secured by the property.
- exchanges: In cases where the owner of a property is going to trade for another property instead of selling it.

How to Estimate Value

What are the steps to the appraisal process?

- Articulate the problem – why is the appraisal being done?
- Decide what information you need.

    -Are there any factors to take into consideration that will help determine the value?

    -What approach should be taken to determine value?

- Identify the highest and best use of the property.
- Determine a ballpark figure of the value of the site.
- Use the market data, cost, and income approaches to identify the property's value.

    -Market data: The appraiser selects comps, usually three that have sold within the past six months, and compare their prices to the property being appraised.

    -Cost: The appraiser estimates how much it will cost to make improvements to the property. This is known as replacement cost. The appraiser may also estimate how much it will cost to create a duplication of the improvements (reproduction cost). This will give the value of the property.

    The land value is also a crucial part in determining the overall property value.

    With the cost approach, it is important to remember that in some cases adjustments may need to be made to take depreciation into consideration. There are three types of depreciation: physical deterioration (general wear and tear), functional obsolescence (features of the property that are no longer ideal), and economic obsolescence (aspects that the owner cannot control, such as economic or environmental influences).

    The formula for determining value using this approach is:

Value = Replacement or Reproduction Cost – Accrued Depreciation + Land Value -

Income: This approach is common in properties that result in income or some other type of revenue.

The first step is to determine the effective gross income which is done so by adding income from all sources and deducting vacancy and collection losses. Next, subtract maintenance and operating expenses. This will give the net operating income. The capitalization rate is what the owner wishes as a return on investment.

The formula is: Value = Net operating income ÷ Capitalization rate

- Reconcile the values arrived at using the different approaches and decide the most probable value.

- Report findings to client using a narrative appraisal report (lengthy, detailed account of findings) or Uniform Residential Appraisal Report (form report typically used for single-family residential appraisals).

What elements establish value?

Demand for the type of property

Utility (desirable use) the property offers

Scarcity of properties available

Transferability of property to a new owner (lack of impediments to a sale)

Terms to remember regarding value:

- Anticipation: The expected worth of the property while owning it and possible gains when selling it.

- Assemblage (plottage): Bringing together adjoining parcels under the same ownership for purposes such as commercial or residential development. This could potentially increase the worth of the parcels.

- Change: Whether physical, political, economical, social or environmental, all properties can be affected by it and result in an increase or decrease of worth.

- Conformity: Generally speaking, properties that are similar to other properties in the neighborhood typically have higher values than those that are not.

- Competition: Can result in higher or lower priced homes, depending on the number of sellers that are brought into the market. If there are a lot of sellers, that may drive the home prices down, while if there are only few sellers, this could be a shortage of properties which could mean higher prices.

- Highest and best use: The maximum use of a property that is legally allowed, which typically produces the most income.

- Law of decreasing returns: When property improvements do not result in an increase in property value.

- Law of increasing returns: When property improvements do result in an increase in property value.

- Progression: The advantage to a property of being located in a desirable area.

- Regression: The disadvantage to a property being located in a less desirable area.

- Substitution: The idea that a buyer does not want to pay more for a property than he would pay for an equivalent property.

- Supply and demand: More properties and less buyers = Lower prices

    Less properties and same/more buyers = Higher prices

Competitive or Comparative Market Analysis (CMA)

In some states, real estate brokers have the authority to prepare property appraisals. In doing so, the broker must be sure to follow the uniform standards as well as inform the potential buyer that the CMA is not an appraisal.

The purpose of the CMA is to allow the homeowner (seller) and potential buyer to have property range of value in a particular area for a certain period of time. With Comparative Market Analysis, properties that have been sold are used. With Competitive Market Analysis, properties that have been sold as well as those that are listed but have not been sold are used.

Given the range of asking/purchase prices of all the properties used, the homeowner (seller) has a more accurate picture of his own realistic home asking price. A seller who asks for more than what is realistic may not attract much interest, which could in turn prevent him from having a buyer. The potential buyer also has an idea of what a fair offer would be. A potential buyer who offers an amount that is lower than what is fair for the property may insult the seller and lose the opportunity to purchase the property or even negotiate with the seller.

Important Contracts/Documents

A contract is executory when the duties under it have not been completely fulfilled. A contract is executed when the duties under it have been completely fulfilled.

The different contracts/documents are:

Listing: Details of agreement between a brokerage and homeowner regarding the sale of a particular property.

Offer to Purchase: Typically in fill-in-the-blank format and displays the terms of the sale of a property (e.g. price). Contingencies are also included.

Purchase & Sale Agreement: Thoroughly explains the responsibilities of each party included in the Offer to Purchase. This document is usually signed once the buyer has completed a home inspection.

Lease: Contract between a renter and owner/manager. The renter is entitled to use the property for the time outlined in the contract (lease).

Deed: Written document that transfers title to real property.

Mortgage note: An IOU that spells out the terms by which the borrower agrees to repays the loan.

Mortgage deed: Explains the collateral (the property) to be used as repayment of debt in case of default.

Bilateral contract: Both parties have responsibilities to fulfill.

Unilateral contract: Only one party has responsibilities to fulfill.

In order to be valid, contracts should:

- Include an offer and acceptance
- Explain the consideration to be used (does not necessarily have to be money)
- Outline the objective, must be legal
- Involve competent parties
- According to the Statute of Frauds, must be in writing (unless lease is for a year or less)
- Signed by both parties, giving their consent

Financing

What is the Cycle of Real Estate?

1. The property is listed

2. The buyer is qualified

3. The buyer is shown the property

4. The agreement between the buyer and seller is signed

5. The buyer finalizes and secures financing

6. The closing occurs

Mortgage Markets

The two types of mortgage markets are primary and secondary. With the primary market, loans are sold directly to borrowers. In the secondary market, the loans that are executed in the primary market are made to investors.

Common purchasers of home loans are:

- The Federal National Mortgage Association (Fannie Mae) – purchases all types of home loans.
- The Federal Home Loan Mortgage Corporation (Freddie Mac) – purchases conventional loans.
- The Government National Mortgage Association (Ginnie Mae) – purchases FHA and VA loans.

Conventional loans: Loans that have no insurance backing from the government. The lender expects the borrower to pay back the loan or endure a foreclosure of the property.

VA-guaranteed loans: Loans that are backed by the Department of Veteran Affairs that the lender will be compensated in the case of the borrower defaulting. In order to be eligible for such a loan, the individual must be a veteran who has been issued a certificate of eligibility by the Department. In addition, the home the borrower wants to buy must be appraised by an appraiser approved by the VA, at which time the VA will issue a certificate of reasonable value. Other stipulations regarding the holders of VA-guaranteed loans are:

- The loan can only be for 1 – 4 family, owner occupied residences.

- There may be a funding fee associated with the loan, depending on the veteran's category and down payment amount. The funding fee is typically 0 – 10%, but can be more.

- Prepayment penalties cannot be assessed with these loans.

- Although the property can be sold at a later time to another veteran or non-veteran, the current borrower must get a "release of liability" notice from the VA so that he/she is not held liable for possible future foreclosure or deficiency.

Federal Housing Administration (FHA) loans: Loans are administered through HUD and protect the lender in case the borrower defaults on the loan.

Stipulations regarding FHA loans are:

- The FHA decides on the maximum amount in loan amounts.

- During closing, the borrower must pay an upfront mortgage insurance premium.

- Prepayment penalties cannot be assessed with these loans.

- The loan can only be for 1 – 4 family, owner occupied residences.

- These loans may be assumed. However, if a new borrower assumes the loan of an existing borrower, both would be responsible in the case of a deficiency due to a foreclosure.

- Lower than normal down payments may be acceptable. However, if the borrower pays less than 20% down payment, he may be required to purchase private mortgage insurance.

Construction loan: Given to a developer or builder on a short-term basis. Funds are received according to construction completion phases. Once built, the builder/developer must obtain long term financing.

Blanket mortgage: A developer or contractor is given funds to purchase several lots of land. With this type of mortgage, a release clause is common, which means the developer/contractor can sell a land parcel while maintaining the mortgage on the rest of the property.

Package mortgage: Personal property and real estate are used as collateral.

Demand mortgage: Allows the lender to require payment whenever it wants to.

Purchase money mortgage: The seller of the property is financing for the buyer.

Junior (second) mortgage: Loan in addition to the primary mortgage. In cases where default occurs, this loan may or may not be paid, depending on whether or not the primary loan is fully paid.

Open-end mortgage: Gives the borrower the option of borrowing additional funds on top of what is initially borrowed, up to a certain amount, without having to complete documentation to rewrite the mortgage.

Wraparound mortgage: Merge a new loan and existing loan. Payment is made on both mortgages to the wraparound mortgagee, who then forwards the payments to the appropriate mortgagee.

Variable (adjustable) rate mortgage: Over the life of the loan, the interest rate can increase or decrease, depending on the Treasury Bill Index. There is a cap set on how much the rate can increase during each rate change period and life of loan.

Balloon loan: Starts of charging a lower than normal fixed-rate loan, but after a certain amount of time, will "balloon". The time at which the loan balloons varies with each lender, but is typically 5, 7, or 10 years. Once the loan balloons, the borrower must pay off the loan.

Shared equity loan: The lender loans the funds at a low interest rate in exchange for a portion of the property's equity.

Equity loan: A second mortgage. It is used to access the equity in the home, to be utilized for making improvements to the property or other reasons.

Negative amortization: The rate of an adjustable rate mortgage increases, but the payment each month stays the same. This results in the payment not being enough to pay the principal and interest, which means the deficit amount is tacked on to the outstanding principal balance.

Term loan: Loan that is interest only. The total loan amount is due at the maturity date of the loan.

Fully amortized loan: Loan that is principal and interest. At the maturity date, the loan will be paid in full.

Partially amortized loan: Loan that is principal and interest. This is short term, so a balloon payment will be made at the maturity date.

Fixed rate loan: Set interest rate over the life of loan. Term, fully amortized and partially amortized loans can include this feature.

How Does the Buyer Secure Financing?

Once the buyer completes a mortgage application, the lender (savings and loan association, commercial bank, mutual savings bank, cooperative bank, credit union, mortgage company, life insurance company, or private lender) completes several steps in deciding whether or not to approve the application. These steps are: 1. Have an appraisal done of the property in question 2. Evaluate the buyer's potential to pay the loan 3. Review the buyer's credit history

Purchase and Sale Agreement forms typically include a financing clause. This means that language is included in the form to protect the buyer in case he does not receive the funding necessary to purchase the property. If funding is not received, he can withdraw his application and receive any earnest money deposits made.

Terms regarding funding

Discount rate: Interest rate charged by the Federal Reserve Bank to financial institutions that loans are made to.

Prime rate: Interest rate charged by banks to preferred borrowers.

Mortgage rates: Rates used for long term loans.

Origination points: Fee paid by borrowers for loan being approved. Each point is 1% of the loan.

Discount points: Paid by the borrower at the start of the loan in order to get a lower interest rate for the life of the loan.

Truth-in-Lending Act: Enacted by Congress in 1968 as a part of the Consumer Protection Act. It is also known as Regulation Z and applies to lenders who conduct more than 25 consumer credit transactions in a year, has more than 5 transactions in a year with a residence used as a security, and/or offers credit to consumers.

Equal Credit Opportunity Act: Creditors are prohibited from discriminating against applicants during credit transactions on the basis of race, color, religion, national origin, sex, marital status, or age.

Home Mortgage Disclosure Act: Financial institutions are required to make annual disclosures about home purchases, refinances, etc. regarding 1 – 4 unit residences.

Community Reinvestment Act: Promotes the idea that commercial banks and savings associations work to help fulfill the financial needs of consumers in all areas, low to high income.

Fair Credit Reporting Act: The collection, disbursement, and utilization of consumer information is regulated via this Act.

Fair and Accurate Credit Transactions Act: Once every twelve months, consumers are able to obtain a free credit report from each of the three credit reporting agencies (Equifax, Experian, and TransUnion).

Gramm-Leach-Billey Act: Financial institutions are required to safeguard the sensitive information of their consumers a well as explain to them the company's information-sharing practices.

Contracts / Agency

Leases

Leases are enforceable when signed by both the landlord and tenant. Leases include a description of the property and do not have to be recorded.

Leases commonly used:

Gross lease: States that the landlord is responsible for paying expenses (i.e. property taxes, insurance, and maintenance costs). Apartment complexes typically use this type of lease.

Net lease: States that the tenant is responsible for paying expenses (i.e. property taxes, insurance, and maintenance costs).

Percentage lease: States that the tenant will pay a percentage of gross sales as rent as well as a base rental amount. This lease is usually used in leases including shopping centers.

Office-building lease: A combination of a gross and net lease. The initial expenses are paid by the landlord, then each tenant pays a pro rata amount of the expenses that exceed that.

Graduated lease: States changes that take place in rent (increase or decrease) over the lease's term.

Ninety-nine year lease: Used in cases like when the owner does not want to sell or the tenant wants to use its funds on capital improvements. Many times used for commercial development.

Leases may be assigned, meaning the individual who originally signed the lease as lessee transfers the entire remaining lease to a third party. Another option for transferring a lease is to sublet, which means only part of the lease is transferred. Whether the original lessee assigns or sublets a lease, the original lessee is still on the hook for the lease being honored. In order to remove the original lessee as responsible, novation must be imitated. Novation is when the original lease is substituted for a new lease. Not all leases allow for the lease to be transferred to another lessee.

What are the Obligations of the Lessor and Lessee?

Lessor:

- Utility services (Lessee typically has to pay for these services, but the lessor must make them available)
- Property that is inhabitable
- Property that does not violate sanitary and/or building codes
- Allow the lessee to have quiet enjoyment of the property
- Not interfere with the lessee's right to a constructive eviction if property is inhabitable or lessor does not allow lessee to have quiet enjoyment of the property
- If collects a security deposit from the lessee (must be deposited into an interest bearing account) and the lessee lives in the apartment for a year or more, the lessee is entitled to the interest paid by the bank (5% or interest paid, whichever is less)

Lessee:

Use the property in the proper manner:

- Keep the property clean
- Use property appliances and fixtures as they are designed to be used
- Do not destroy property or allow others to do so

Options

An option allows an individual to purchase a property at a certain amount if done so within a specified timeframe. Options are created by the property owner bring paid cash and putting the option in writing. Options are assignable without approval from the property owner.

Purchase and Sale Agreement

There are several key elements included on the Purchase and Sale Agreement to make it valid. These are:

- The names of all parties involved

- A land description
- The sales price
- The amount of earnest money provided by the buyer
- The contract date
- Buyer and seller signatures

The Indiana Statute of Frauds says that the Purchase and Sale Agreements must be in writing. The exception to this rule is for a lease that will be enforced for a year or less from the contract date. Once signed, the buyer has equitable title, which means he has interest in the property even though the transaction is not fully complete. Once the transaction is fully complete, the buyer has legal title to the property which gives him all of the rights associated with it.

The majority of Purchase and Sale Agreements give buyers the "right to assign", which means they can assign the contract to someone else, however, they are not off the hook for the requirements of the contract in the case where the new assignee does not fulfill his duties under the contract.

Breach of Contract

A breach of contract is when one party of a contract fails to uphold his duties outlined in the contract. When this occurs, the party who is aggrieved can be compensated by doing the following:

- Suing for monetary damages
- Suing for the party who breached the contract to fulfill his duties under the contract
- If the seller is the one wronged, he can sue for liquidated money damages (i.e. keeping the earnest money deposit)
- Both parties agreeing to annul the contract

Termination of an Offer

A purchase offer can be terminated if one of the following conditions exists:

- Either of the parties dies
- The timeframe of the offer expires

- The offeror revokes before being informed that the offeree accepts
- Either party becomes bankrupt
- The property is destroyed or condemned
- The offeree rejects a counteroffer

Counteroffers are used in response to the initial offer regarding the sale/purchase of a property. The individual to whom the counteroffer is made may immediately agree with the counteroffer or further negotiate until a mutually agreed upon offer is reached.

Valid/void/voidable contracts

Valid contract: Legal, binding and enforceable.

Void contract: Not legal, binding, or enforceable.

Voidable contract: Binding for one party but not the other.

Agency Law

An agent is the one who represents the fiduciary interest of his/her client. There are two types of agencies: single and dual. In a single agency, the agent works on behalf of either the buyer or seller. In a dual agency, the agent works on behalf of the buyer and seller. In the case of a dual agency in the state of Indiana, the agent must have written consent from the buyer and seller that they are aware of and agree to arrangement. The agent (in a dual agency situation) cannot offer all fiduciary duties to both clients.

The fiduciary duties are:

Obedience

Loyalty

Disclosure (of material facts concerning the transaction)

Confidentiality

Accountability (of funds)

Reasonable care

A real estate company can either be set up so that all agents in the company have the same relationship with the customer OR only the agent listed on the disclosure form can represent the customer.

In Indiana, there are several relationship options between the agent and potential buyer or seller. These are:

- Seller's agent – Represents the seller in all aspects of the transaction and owes all fiduciary duties to the seller.

- Buyer's agent – Represents the buyer in all aspects of the transaction and owes all fiduciary duties to the buyer.

- Facilitator – Brings the buyer and seller together but does not act on behalf of either party as agent. Does not owe fiduciary duties to either party.

- Designated seller's and buyer's agent – Represents his/her client (either the buyer or seller) and owes all fiduciary duties to client. If the client agrees, the agent can be "designated" as the client's only agent. In Indiana, this must be in writing.

- Dual agent – Represents the buyer and seller. All fiduciary duties cannot be given to either party. In Indiana, this must be in writing and signed by both the buyer and seller. Also in Indiana, it is unlawful to have an undisclosed dual agency.

Listing Types

Open: States that the broker will get paid a commission if (s)he secures a buyer, which results in the sale of the property. This can be done between a seller and as many brokers (s)he would like. If the listing broker does not sell the home, but rather the homeowner or another broker, the listing broker does not get paid the commission.

Exclusive agency: The seller can only enter into agreement to sell with one broker. If the broker actively sells the house or the house is sold through MLS, the broker will be paid the commission. If the homeowner sells the house on his own, he will not pay commission to the broker.

Exclusive right to sell: States the listing broker will receive the commission on the sale of the property regardless of who actually sells it.

Net: States that the homeowner will receive a specific amount from the sale of the property. Anything received over that amount will go to the listing broker. This type of arrangement is illegal in Indiana.

Multiple listing service (MLS): System used to display information all members have with regard to real estate property they have for sale.

Termination of Agency

Agency contracts can be terminated by:

- completion of the objective
- time limit expiration
- rescission
- revocation
- death of the principal or broker
- property destruction
- bankruptcy of either party

How are agents paid?

Agents guarantee payment for services by working under some type of agreement (i.e. contract, listing agreement, or buyer-agency representation agreement).

According to *Tristam's Landing versus Wait* decision, the broker who is entitled to the commission is the one who has "procured a ready, willing, and able buyer."

What is a commission split?

When properties are sold, the commission paid for the sale is dividing among many parties. This can include a co-broker, broker-owner, and agent. Different real estate offices choose different ways to split the commission. For example, some offices take off the top a fee that covers operating expenses, while others may charge the agent a set monthly fee that takes care of overhead.

Licensing requirements in Indiana

Read – Indiana Professional Licensing Agency: http://www.in.gov/pla/2788.htm

What does the Real Estate Commission do?

The Commission, which is appointed by the governor, consists of 12 members. Nine are people who have significant experience as real estate licensees. Two are people with a "recognized interest in consumer affairs," and cannot be a real estate professional. There is also one "at large" member. The chairperson of the Commission (one of the six members) is also appointed by the governor.

Every member of the Commission serves for five years. The Commission must meet at least monthly and must have four members present to have a quorum and conduct business.

The Indiana Board has the authority to do many things:

- Carry out state law.
- Administer examinations.
- Review records.
- Enforce license law by having hearings and if necessary, appeals.
- Give, refuse, and revoke licenses

When would an agent's license be temporarily or permanently taken away or refused for a renewal? If he:

- Willingly makes misrepresentations
- Serves as broker and undisclosed principal in one transaction
- Serves as a dual agent without receiving written permission from the buyer and seller
- Does not account for received funds within an acceptable timeframe
- Compensates an unlicensed individual with a commission
- Does not report a criminal conviction
- Provided false information on the initial license application or renewal form
- Engages in real estate activities with an expired license
- Engages in real estate activities while in an impaired state
- Participates in a net listing

- Participates in discriminatory practices
- Does not supply a real estate contract copy to all of the appropriate parties
- Commingles business and personal funds
- Encourages a party of a contract to break it in order to benefit himself
- Receives, gives, or charges a hidden fee on expenses for a principal

If there is a hearing with regard to an agent's license, records and witnesses may be permissible. The licensee must be informed about the hearing (in a written format) a minimum of ten days before the hearing is scheduled to be held. If the licensee appears for the hearing, he/she can be represented by counsel. (S)he can also ask questions of witnesses present. If the licensee is not satisfied with the decision of the Board, an appeal to the superior court within twenty days is acceptable. If in the end, the licensee still loses his/her license, (s)he has seven days to release it to the Board.

There are many activities in Indiana, as related to real-estate that require a license to perform when a fee is charged. These include:

- sales
- exchanges
- purchases
- rentals/leases
- negotiates
- offers
- listing
- options
- advertise real property
- prospecting
- loan negotiating
- apartment search

What activities do not require a real estate license?

- Person acting on his/her own behalf
- Property manager employed by property owner
- Auctioneer who is licensed as such
- Trustee
- Public servant executing official duties
- Attorney-in-fact under power of attorney
- Court appointee

- Financial institution employees (bank, insurance company, or credit union)

What Are the Types of Licenses?

Real Estate Broker: For a fee, this individual performs the above activities for another person.

Real Estate Salesperson: Individual cannot perform negotiations but can perform the above activities. A salesperson must always work under the cover of an employer broker. If the salesperson is a non-resident, she can hold an Indiana real estate license, but is required to file a power of attorney designating the chairman of the Board as attorney in fact. This is necessary in case the salesperson has any legal actions against her.

What Makes One Eligible for Licensing?

An individual is eligible for a salesperson license if he:

- Is at least 18 years old
- Fulfills 54 hours of approved coursework OR has completed at least 8 hours of approved college or university coursework and received a waiver
- Pays the $40.50 application fee
- Pays the $61 exam fee
- Successfully completes the exam
- Agrees to and passes a background check
- Has no convictions for crimes that indicate "untrustworthy" behavior
- Applies for a license within 120 days of passing the exam

An individual salesperson is eligible for an Associate Broker or Broker's license if he:

- Is at least 18 years old
- Is a resident of Indiana
- Is a licensed salesperson and has been in active status for at least one year
- Fulfills 54 hours of approved coursework
- Pays the application fee of $65.50

If a licensed broker (also the sole proprietor) of a real estate agency dies, the broker's representative must apply with the Commission and will be issued a temporary license. The completion of an exam is not necessary. The license is non-renewal and good up to one year from the date of the original broker's death.

Under normal circumstances, a real estate license is valid for two years. It must be renewed before December 31 the renewal year. Salesperson licenses expire on December 31 of odd-numbered years, and broker licenses expire on December 21 of even-numbered years. Before renewing the license (within the two year period), brokers and salespersons must complete 16 continuing education hours. The continuing education requirement may be waived for practitioners who are serving in the armed forces or who have an incapacitating illness. Practitioners wishing for a waiver must apply. Brokers and salespersons that do not complete the continuing education courses will have their licenses put in an "inactive status". With an "inactive" license, individuals can earn and collect referral fees, but cannot practice real estate. In addition to completing continuing education course hours, to renew a license, individuals must pay the renewal fee.

Indiana has real estate license reciprocity with 14 states: Arkansas, Colorado, Connecticut, Florida, Georgia, Illinois, Iowa, Kentucky, Massachusetts, Mississippi, Missouri, Nebraska, Oklahoma, and Wisconsin. An applicant originally licensed in any of these states may apply for licensing by reciprocity in Indiana by filling out the application and paying the $40.50 fee.

Statutory Requirements Governing Activities of Licenses

Advertising requirements:

- Misleading or false advertising is prohibited by brokers

- Advertising without disclosing the fact that the broker is a real estate broker is forbidden

- Advertising property under the salesperson's name is not allowed

- Advertising that's done in a way that directly or indirectly discriminates against any group is prohibited

Salespersons cannot be self-employed, but must be hired by a real estate broker as an employee or independent contractor. Brokers can compensate salespersons via payment, fees, or commissions. Brokers are responsible for the actions of their salespersons.

Brokers are also responsible for maintaining a place of business and making the Board aware of any changes regarding location. A copy of the broker's license must be displayed in an area of the office that is visible to the public. In addition, the broker must let the Board know all of the agents affiliated with the firm. If an agent leaves, the Board must be informed…if a new agent joins the firm, the Board must be informed.

Clients should not be advised by the agent to avoid securing the representation of an attorney at any point of the transaction.

Indiana and Promotional Sales of Out-of-State Real Property

- Real property located in a state other than Indiana cannot be offered as property in Indiana unless the developer of the property registers with the Department of Housing and Urban Development (HUD). Registering includes filling out the appropriate paperwork, paying the appropriate fee, and annually renewing the registration.

- If an out-of-state property is registered in Indiana, this must be noted in all of the property's advertisements in Indiana.

- Out-of-state properties registered with the Board in Indiana must be offered and sold by a broker who is licensed in Indiana.

- An Indiana broker must notify the board within seven days of taking on the client if he/she is working for the owner/developer of an out-of-state property.

Apartment rentals in Indiana

When renting an apartment in Indiana, brokers and salespersons are required by law to supply the prospective tenant with written notification of whether or not the potential tenant is required to pay a fee for services rendered. If a fee is required, the notice will also indicate how much the fee is, when it should be paid, as well as whether or not the potential tenant will receive all or some of it back if a tenancy is not established. The notification must be supplied the first time the salesperson or broker and potential tenant meet face-to-face. The notice should include the signature and date of the salesperson or broker and potential tenant, and the salesperson or broker's license number. If the potential tenant does not agree to signing the notice, the salesperson / broker must indicate this on the notice.

Three years is the time period in which the salesperson/broker must keep the notice on file, and if required by the Board or other appropriate agents, should be available upon request.

Other information brokers should keep on file for three years are rental listings and other written notification of available apartments. This is from the date the apartment is rented. Checks, money orders, receipts, etc. should be filed for three years from the date of issuance.

All advertisements regarding an apartment available for rent should also include the statement, "The apartment advertised may no longer be available for rental."

Sherman Anti-Trust Act

The Sherman Anti-Trust Act prohibits many business practices that could unfairly restrict marketplace free competition. Some of these include:

- No price fixing
- Real estate companies cannot offer services in only particular geographical areas
- Real estate companies cannot consciously direct business away from other real estate companies
- Salespersons/brokers cannot create organizations that unfairly exclude qualified brokers from having access to marketing and sales information.

Settlement and the Conveyance of Property

Settlement procedures: Who brings/does what?

Seller:

- Deed
- Current property tax certificates
- Insurance policies
- Termite inspections
- Survey maps
- Keys, garage door openers, etc.

Additional documents that the seller may have to provide in the case of selling an income-producing property, include:

- Leases
- Operating statements
- Estoppel letters from the tenants

- Maintenance contracts

Buyer:

- Monies (good funds)
- Survey
- Insurance policy
- Flood insurance policy
- Termite certificate

The closing agent/officer:

- Ensure signatures are correctly executed
- Make sure copies are made and distributed to appropriate parties involved
- Issue checks, if applicable
- Forward the deed to be recorded

Attorneys for the buyer and seller may be present at the closing.

All applicable disclosures must be presented at closing (e.g. Lead-based paint).

Before closing takes place, the majority of lenders require a termite inspection of the property, appraisal, and proof that the buyer has insurance that covers the property in the case of fire, flood, casualty, or wind damage. This all done to ensure that the property is sufficient collateral.

Purpose of closing/settlement

Right before the closing takes place, the buyer and his broker (if applicable) do a final walk-through of the property to make sure it is in the condition agreed upon by the seller and buyer.

Real Estate Settlement and Procedures Act

Consumers complained about closing costs with regard to purchasing real estate as well as the procedures associated with purchasing real estate. As a result, the Real Estate Settlement and Procedures Act (RESPA) was passed.

RESPA refers to residential transactions that involve first mortgage loans made on 1 – 4 family residences, cooperatives, and condominiums.

With RESPA, it's important to remember several key acts that are illegal:

- Fees paid for services not rendered and kickbacks are strictly prohibited under the Act.
- Also prohibited is the requirement of buyers to purchase title insurance from a specific title company.
- The amount of advance property tax and insurance payments lenders can require of borrowers must be no more than 1/6 or 2 months' worth of annual property taxes.

Deeds

The deed is the legal document used to show a transfer of ownership from the seller (grantor) to the buyer (grantee). Deeds do not have to be recorded to be valid, but if they are recorded, they are done so through the county registry of deeds. This gives a constructive notice of the transfer of ownership.

There are three main types of deeds used, including general warranty, special warranty, and quit claim deed, however, only the quit claim deed is used in Indiana.

General warranty deed: Includes the expressed or implied word from the grantor about the title's validity.

Special warranty: Includes word from the grantor regarding the state of the title once he obtained ownership.

Quit claim deed: Grantor conveys interest that he has in property but does not give word regarding warranty of said property.

Other deeds that are used include:

Sheriff's deed: Transfers title of property after it being auctioned off due to foreclosure or some other court-related action.

Tax deed: Transfers title of property sold at an auction to take care of unpaid taxes.

Gift deed: Does not require consideration in order to be paid by the grantee.

There are several key elements included in the deed to make it valid. These are:

- Identification of all parties involved

- "Granting clause"
- Consideration
- Details of the rights transferred
- Legal property description
- Correct execution
- Grantor must state the deed is his "free act and deed" and notarize if the deed is to be recorded at the registry of deeds

Torrens System

The Torrens System, also known as Land Court, is used to register land. Most land in Indiana is recorded, but some is registered. The title of registered land is searched by the Land Court. In the case of registered land, the owner is provided with a certificate of title instead of a deed.

Referencing Documents

There are two types of indexing systems, and either may be used in Indiana. These are the tract index and the alphabetical index.

For the **tract index**, each parcel of land is identified on a map. Each parcel is numbered. The number refers to a page number in a reference book. The book lists all other documents filed for the parcel of land can be found.

The **alphabetical system**, also referred to as the **grantor-grantee index**, is an alphabetical listing of all properties that changed hands during a given calendar year. To use this index, you will need the name of the buyer or seller of the piece of land you want to research. You can then use this information to find the type of document filed on the property, as well as the reference book and page number where it can be found.

Indiana Taxes

Indiana does not charge transfer tax when real property is transferred from one to another. There may be a charge for the tax assessor processing the deed.

Indiana does not charge state intangible tax on the buyer's new mortgage.

Laws Regarding Fair Housing and Consumer Protection

Federal

Federal Civil Rights Act of 1866: Regarding individual home sellers and real estate agencies, they are not allowed to racially discriminate against anyone when it comes to selling, leasing, or any other activities with real or personal property.

Federal Fair Housing Act of 1968 (Title VIII): The discrimination of individuals based on sex, race, color, religion, national origin, handicap, and familial status is strictly prohibited with regard to the sale or rental of housing or vacant land.

Acts that are prohibited:

- Choosing not to sell or rent to someone who is in a protected class. Protected classes include color, race, religion/creed, ancestry / national origin, gender, handicap, or familial status.

- Modifying services or conditions for different people as a way of discriminating against someone in a protected class.

- Advertising in such a way that discriminates against someone in a protected class, which would therefore prevent the sale or rental of a residence.

- Dishonestly telling an individual that a property is unavailable, as a way of discriminating against them.

- Blockbusting: Making money by encouraging homeowners to rent or sell their properties by telling them individuals of a protected class are moving into their neighborhood.

- Redlining: Changing the terms of a home loan of a person in a protected class as a way of discriminating against them.

- Preventing individuals from full participation in organizations that engage in the rental or sale of residences (e.g. multiple listing service).

- Steering: Encouraging individuals to gravitate toward or away from certain neighborhoods based on protected class.

- Stating in an appraisal report that the value of a property is impacted by any of the above prohibited activities.

- Including notes with discriminatory preferences.

- Negatively interfering with anyone who is exercising his rights.

Additional Information About Protected Classes Covered:

Familial status deals with preventing discrimination against children or families with children.

Discriminating against handicapped (mentally and physically) persons by not making reasonable accommodations regarding policies or necessary changes to the premises is prohibited.

Since 1991, homes that are four-family or larger are required to be handicapped accessible for first floor units. In homes where elevators are present, units on upper floors must also be handicap accessible.

The 1968 Federal Fair Housing Act covers residential property.

What does Title VIII Not Cover?

- The sale or rental by an individual who owns three or less properties and does not use a broker, engage in discriminatory advertising, and have not sold another property in the last two years.

- The rental of rooms in an owner-occupied, multi-family home with two or four units, providing no salesperson is used and he has not engaged in discriminatory advertising.

- The sale or rental of a property by a religious organization to a person of the same religion (for non-commercial purposes), providing no prohibited restrictions are enforced.

- The rental of properties managed by a private club for members for purposes other than commercial.

- Elderly housing that meets particular HUD rules.

Individuals who believe they have been discriminated against can file a complaint with HUD or civil action with the court.

If it is proven that the individuals have indeed been discriminated against, the offender may face penalties such as civil penalties, monetary fines, and court costs, among other things.

Indiana State General Law

Indiana Fair Housing Law

In Indiana, there are two protected class categories: 1. Based on race, color, religion, national origin, ancestry, sex, age, or disability and 2. Familial status (presence of children under 18 years of age).

Category 1

There are some exemptions to this law regarding home sellers, but not real estate agencies. These exemptions become void if discriminatory advertising has taken place. The exemptions:

- When an owner-occupied, two-family residence is being leased
- If the housing is designated "elderly housing" and it receives state or federal funding, it is exempt based only on age.
- If a community is an authorized "55+" community and is situated on at least 10 acres, it is exempt based only on age.

Category 2

Not agreeing to rent or sell to someone solely because they have children is illegal. This also includes not renting to someone with children because the owner knows the property has lead paint or other safety violations they are not willing to get up to code. Discrimination advertising is never allowed, neither is advertising that is different for people with or without children. As with Category 1 under the Indiana Fair Housing Act, there are exemptions to this rule:

- If the residence is a three-family or less residence and there is an elderly or ill resident for whom allowing children to live on the premises would be a hardship.
- The lease is a temporary owner/occupant lease.
- The lease is for an owner-occupied two-family residence.

It is also a violation of fair housing standards to refuse credit services or rental accommodations to someone solely because he or she receives public assistance, rental assistance, or housing subsidy.

Individuals in any one of these categories who feel they have been discriminated against can file a complaint with the Indiana Commission on Equal Opportunity or civil action with the court.

If it is proven that the individuals have indeed been discriminated against, they can be compensated in a variety of ways such as affirmative relief or civil penalties.

If it is determined that a real estate agent is in violation of this law, he may have his license suspended or revoked.

Indiana Uniform Deceptive Trade Practices Act (UDTPA)

This law applies to salespeople and brokers and forbids deceptive and unfair trade practices. Violation of the law can result in being sued for a maximum of triple damages and attorney's fees.

Lead Paint Law

There is a federal and state law that real estate agents must abide by regarding lead paint disclosure requirements.
For homes built before 1978, the prospective buyer must be provided with a Department of Public Health Property Transfer Notification Certification that informs the buyer of whether or not the seller is aware of lead paint anywhere on the property. The seller must provide reports about it. The buyer then has ten days to have a test completed to check for lead paint. This process is done before the prospective buyer signs a Purchase and Sale Agreement.

If the prospective buyer decides he would like to continue with the purchase, he must be given a Lead Paint Notification and Tenant Certificate Form. Also, if the new tenant has a child who lives in the property that is under the age of 6, the current owner must de-lead.

Additionally, potential hazards such as those regarding smoke detectors must also be addressed. Within 60 days of closing on the property, the fire department must inspect and issue a smoke detector certificate saying the smoke detectors in the property are sufficient and properly working. Homes that are three-family or larger must also have hard-wired smoke detectors in common areas of the home. Homes that are six-family or larger must have hard-wired smoke detectors everywhere in the property.

With regard to commercial properties, a 21E certificate is used to endorse the fact that the property has been cleared for all hazardous waste.

Management of Property

Condominiums

Condominiums in Indiana are governed by the Indiana Horizontal Property Act. Units can be owned by an individual fee simple estate, which means in the case of payment default, only that individual owner is penalized, not all other owners.

The condominium master deed explains details of the property, each unit, and land and common area percentage ownership for each buyer. In addition to the master deed, a unit deed exists. A unit deed is provided each time the sale of a unit takes place. The unit deed includes bylaws, by which each owner agrees to abide by. The bylaws describe the condominium association and its legal authority.

There are typically fees associated with condominium ownership that are paid monthly. The amount due depends on the percentage of ownership for each owner.

Common areas of the condominium are for the use of each owner, unless designated as a limited common element (e.g. balcony).

If a condominium owner fails to pay monthly condominium fees, a priority lien may be assessed against the property, under the Super Lien Bill. Priority liens take precedence over first mortgage holder liens.

The transfer of ownership of a condominium in Indiana must follow this process: (1) The current owner must obtain a certified letter from the condominium association. This document states that all condominium fees have been paid through the end of that current month. (2) The current owner must obtain an insurance certificate that proves that the new owner and his mortgage holder will be protected by the condominium master insurance policy.

Cooperatives

Cooperatives are unlike condominiums in they have one owner, a corporation. There is a blanket mortgage on the property. The corporation is responsible for paying ad valorem taxes.

The buyers of each unit are considered stockholders, as once they make the purchase, they are given a stock certificate in the corporation. With ownership, the buyer has a "proprietary unit lease" which means they can occupy the property for the life of the corporation.

The downside to ownership in a cooperative as opposed to a condominium is that if one shareholder defaults on his monthly payment, the other shareholder tenants are affected and they must come together to make up the shortage.

Time Sharing

Time sharing is just as its name states. Several owners share interest in one condominium with the right to occupy the property for a certain amount of time each year. All owners pay costs such as maintenance and management fees. The actual amounts depend on the ownership period and total number of available ownership periods. Time share ownership can be fee simple or lease-hold interest. Another option with time shares is an exchange program, where owners can exchange their time share credits for the occupation of other locations.

Subdivisions

"Subdivision" is used to describe when large tracts of land are divided into smaller parcels that will be for sale. The land is improved (added infrastructure, etc.) and typically regulated by local, state, and federal law. The plat will be recorded, showing lots, blocks, etc.

If the subdivision includes greater than 25 lots, exceeding 20 acres and are offered for sale, crossing state lines, HUD (Federal Interstate Land Sales Full Disclosure Act) requires that several reports be filed.

Real Estate Math

The Real Estate Math section of this guide should not be taken lightly. Most state exams include around 10% math questions, but you don't have to be a mathematician to effectively complete this part. Use this review to refresh your understanding of or learn arithmetic, algebra, geometry, and word problems. You will also have the opportunity to practice with the included sample problems for each math topic.

Some of the math question types you may come across on your exam include:

- Area
- Percents
- Property tax
- Loan-to-Value Ratios
- Points
- Equity
- Qualifying Buyers
- Prorations
- Commissions
- Proceeds from sales
- Transfer Tax/Conveyance Tax/Revenue Stamps
- Competitive Market Analyses
- Income Properties
- Depreciation

Use the following to help you complete the math questions.

Tips for Completing Math Questions

Before taking the exam, and specifically before completing the math portion of the exam, there are a few things you may want to keep in mind:

Leave No Question Unanswered

Although you may not know the answer to every question right off the top of your head, it is advisable that you answer every question to the best of your ability. You immediately have a 1 in 4 chance of getting the answer correct. There are also some instances where an answer choice is clearly not correct, which betters your chance for selecting the right answer.

Use a Calculator

You must confirm with the testing center before taking the exam, but some states allow the use of a calculator. However, you shouldn't solely rely on the calculator as this can slow you down, but using it to work out some mathematical equations can prove to be very helpful.

Utilize Scrap Paper

Let nothing take the place of scrap paper. While using a calculator can help you get the answer quickly, writing your thought process on scrap paper provides information for you to refer to in case you get stuck.

Review! Review! Review!

Avoiding an incorrect answer can be something as simple as checking your work.

Math Review

Basic math skills in the areas of arithmetic, algebra, geometry, and word problems will be necessary. Here's a review.

Arithmetic

Multiplication

"Factor" is the term used to describe the two numbers that are being multiplied. The answer is known as the product.

Example:

2 x 5 = 10   2 and 5 are the factors. 10 is the product.

A multiplication problem can be presented in a variety of ways.

- You may see a dot between the two factors, which denotes multiplication:
  $2 \cdot 5 = 10$

- The use of parentheses around a part of one or more factors denotes multiplication:
  (2)5 = 10

  2(5) = 10

  (2)(5) = 10

- A number next to a variable denotes multiplication:
  2a = 10

  Multiply "2" and "a" to arrive at the product of 10.

Division

The divisor is the number "divided by"; while the dividend is the number the divisor is going into. The result is the quotient.

Division is similar to multiplication by the fact that there are several ways to present the problem.

12÷3 = 4

12/3 = 4

$\frac{12}{3} = 4$

Decimals

The key to understanding decimals is knowing each place value.

Here is a table to help you remember:

4	6	3	2	6	.	5	7	9	1

Ten Thousands	Thousands	Hundreds	Tens	Ones	Decimal	Tenths	Hundredths	Thousandths	Ten Thousandths

Using the above table, this number would be expressed as: 46,326.5791

It is also important to understand how to round decimals. If the number immediately following the number you must round is 5 or greater, you increase the preceding number by 1. If the number immediately following the number you must round is less than 5, drop that number and leave the preceding number as is.

Example:

0.236 = 0.24

0.234 = 0.23

Adding Fractions

Adding fractions with like denominators is a simple operation. You add the numerators together and leave the denominator as it appears.

Example:

$$\frac{3}{5} + \frac{1}{5} = \frac{4}{5}$$

Adding fractions with unlike denominators requires you to find the least common denominator. The least common denominator is the smallest number that each of your denominators can divide into evenly.

Example:

$\frac{4}{6} + \frac{3}{4}$ The least common denominator is 12 because 6 x 2 = 12 and 4 x 3 = 12.

Once you have determined the least common denominator, each fraction should be converted to its new form. This is done by multiplying the numerator and denominator by the appropriate number in order to arrive at the least common denominator. Next, you add the new numerators, which gives you the final answer.

Example:

$$\frac{4}{6} + \frac{3}{4} = \frac{2(4)}{2(6)} + \frac{3(3)}{3(4)} = \frac{8}{12} + \frac{9}{12} = \frac{17}{12}$$

Subtracting Fractions

Subtracting fractions with like denominators is a simple operation. You subtract the numerators and leave the denominator as it appears.

Example:

$$\frac{3}{5} - \frac{1}{5} = \frac{2}{5}$$

Subtracting fractions with unlike denominators requires you to find the least common denominator. The least common denominator is the smallest number that each of your denominators can divide into evenly.

Example:

$\frac{8}{9} - \frac{3}{6}$ The least common denominator is 18 because 9 x 2 = 18 and 6 x 3 = 18.

Once you have determined the least common denominator, each fraction should be converted to its new form. This is done by multiplying the numerator and denominator by the appropriate number in order to arrive at the least common denominator. Next, you subtract the new numerators, which gives you the final answer.

Example:

$$\frac{8}{9} - \frac{3}{6} = \frac{2(8)}{2(9)} - \frac{3(3)}{3(6)} = \frac{16}{18} - \frac{9}{18} = \frac{7}{18}$$

Multiplying Fractions

When multiplying fractions, the denominators of the fractions can be alike or different. Either way, the operation is performed the same.

Multiply the numerators and denominators.

Example:

$$\frac{4}{7} \times \frac{3}{5} = \frac{12}{35}$$

Dividing Fractions

When dividing fractions, you actually multiply the fractions by their reciprocals.

You find the reciprocal of a number by turning it upside down. For example, the reciprocal of $\frac{3}{8}$ is $\frac{8}{3}$.

Solve the problem.

$$\frac{18}{24} \div \frac{2}{4} = \frac{18}{24} \times \frac{4}{2} = \frac{72}{48} = \frac{3}{2}$$

Percent

"Percent" is used to describe a portion of a whole, with the whole being 100.

How do I change a decimal to a percentage?

This operation is simple. Move the decimal two places to the right of the number, add a percentage sign, and voila!

Example:

.32 = 32%

.04 = 4%

.1 = 10%

How do I change a fraction to a percentage?

The first step in converting a fraction to a percentage is to change the fraction to a decimal. Do so by dividing the denominator into the numerator. From here you move the decimal two places to the right of the number, and then add the percentage sign.

Example:

$\frac{3}{6}$ = .5 = 50%

$\frac{1}{4}$ = .25 = 25%

How do I change a percentage to a decimal?

Simply slide the decimal two places to the left of the number and take away the percentage symbol.

Example:

69% = .69

4% = .04

How do I change a percentage to a fraction?

Divide the number by 100. Reduce to lowest terms.

Example:

$25\% = \frac{25}{100} = \frac{1}{4}$

$62\% = \frac{62}{100} = \frac{31}{50}$

How do I change a percentage that is greater than 100 to a decimal or mixed fraction?

To change to a decimal:

Add a decimal point two places to the left of the number –

298% = 2.98

600% = 6.0

980% = 9.8

To change to a mixed fraction –

$275\% = \frac{275}{100} = \frac{200}{100} + \frac{75}{100} = 2 + \frac{3}{4} = 2\frac{3}{4}$

$275\% = 2\frac{3}{4}$

$550\% = \frac{550}{100} = \frac{500}{100} + \frac{50}{100} = 5 + \frac{1}{2} = 5\frac{1}{2}$

$550\% = 5\frac{1}{2}$

Conversions Commonly Seen in Real Estate:

Fraction	Decimal	Percentage
½	.5	50%
¼	.25	25%
1/3	.333…	33.3…%
2/3	.666…	66.6…%
1/10	.1	10%
1/8	.125	12.5%
1/6	.1666…	16.6…%
1/5	.2	20%

Algebra

Equations

To solve an equation, you must determine that is equal to the unidentified variable.

Things to remember about equations:

- There are two parts to an equation. They are separated by an equal sign.
- An operation performed in an equation must be done in each part.
- When beginning to solve the equation, priority #1 is to get the variables on one side and numbers on the other.
- You will usually have to divide both parts of the equation using the coefficient. This will enable the variable to equal an exact number.

How do I check an equation to make sure it is correct?

Once you've solved the equation, take the number equal to the variable and input into the original equation.

Example:

x = 15

Original equation: $\dfrac{x}{3} = \dfrac{x+35}{10}$

$\dfrac{15}{3} = \dfrac{15+35}{10}$

$\dfrac{15}{3} = \dfrac{50}{10}$

5 = 5

Algebraic Fractions

Example:

How do I solve subtraction on two fractions with different denominators?

$\dfrac{x}{6} - \dfrac{x}{12}$

$\dfrac{x(2)}{6(2)} - \dfrac{x}{12}$

$\dfrac{2x}{12} - \dfrac{x}{12} = \dfrac{x}{12}$

Geometry

Terms to remember:

- **Area** – Refers to the space inside a two-dimensional figure.
- **Circumference** – Refers to the linear distance around a circle.
- **Perimeter** – Refers to the total distance around a two-dimensional figure.
- **Radius** – Refers to the distance from the center point of a circle to its perimeter.

Area

Area refers to the space inside a two-dimensional figure.

In the triangle below, the area is the part that is shaded green.

 = Area

Area Formulas for Various Shapes

Circle: $A = \pi r^2$

Sphere: $A = 4\pi r^2$

Rectangle: $A = lw$

Square: $A = s^2$

Triangle: $A = \frac{1}{2} bh$

Parallelogram: $A = bh$

What do the above letters/symbols mean?

A: Area

π: 3.14

r: Radius

l: Length

w: Width

s: Side length

b: Base

h: Height

Examples of area:

Area of circle   **Area of rectangle**

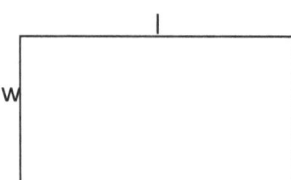

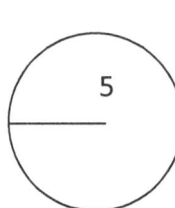   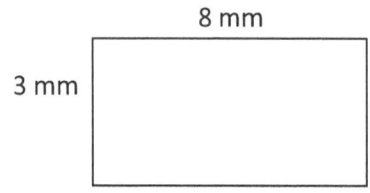

$A = \pi r^2$ $A = lw$

$A = \pi \times (5 \times 5)$ $A = 8mm \times 3mm = 24\ mm^2$

$A = \pi \times 25$

$A = 3.14 \times 25$

$A = 78.54$

Perimeter

Perimeter refers to the total distance around a two-dimensional figure.

It is simply calculated by adding together all of the sides of the figure.

Example:

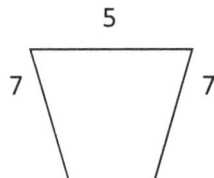

Perimeter = 7 + 7 + 5 + 3 = 22

Circumference is the perimeter of a circle.

Formula for circumference: $C = 2\pi r$

Word Problems

Understanding word problems is crucial to doing well on the math problems of the Real Estate Exam, as these make up a significant portion of the math problems found on the exam.

Before knowing how to solve the problems, you must understand what the problem is asking.

Terms you will commonly see:

- **Increase**
  What operation do you perform?

  Answer: Addition

  Example:

  A number is increased by 7, which means $x + 7$.

- **Less than**
  What operation do you perform?

  Answer: Subtraction

Example:

A number less than 12, which means 12 − x.

- **Product or times**
  What operation do you perform?

  Answer: Multiplication

  Example:

  A number times 8, which means x(8).

- **Times the sum**
  What operation do you perform?

  Answer: Multiply a number by a quantity

  Example:

  Six times the sum of nine and a number, which is 6(9 + x).

- **Of**
  What operation do you perform?

  Answer: Multiplication

  Example:

  5% of 100 is 5, which means 5% × 100 = 5.

- **Is**

  What operation do you perform?

  Answer: Equals

  Example:

  10 is 20 minus 10, which means 10 = 20 − 10.

- **The use of two variables**

  What operation do you perform?

  Answer: Whatever the equation states

  Example:

  A number y exceeds 3 times a number x by 8, which means $y = 3x + 8$.

Creating and Using Variables in Word Problems

In order to solve some word problems, you may be required to create and use variables. The first step in doing so is to determine what you know and don't know regarding the equation.

Examples:

Perry made $5 more dollars than Billy in his paper route.

What do you know? Perry made $5 more

What don't you know? The amount that Billy made

So,

The amount Billy made is x and the amount Perry made is x + 5.

Pam made 3 times as many A's on her report card as Jan.

What do you know? Pam made 3 times as many A's as Jan

What don't you know? The number of A's that Jan made

So,

The number A's Jan made is x and the number of A's Pam made is 3x.

Greg has 4 more than 2 times the number of marbles that Shelly has.

What do you know? Greg has 4 more than 2 times the number of marbles Shelly has

What don't you know? The number of marbles Shelly has

So,

The number of marbles Shelly has is x and the number of marbles Greg has 2x + 4.

Percentage Word Problems

There are three main types of percentage word problems. All three types follow the same formula for calculating the result.

Formula:

$$\frac{\text{part}}{\text{whole}} = \frac{\%}{100}$$

Calculate the problem substituting the appropriate information in the above formula.

Keep this in mind:

- On the percentage side, 100 will always be the denominator.
- If you are not provided with a percentage amount to use as the numerator, use a variable.
- On the number side, the number always equals the whole (100%). In the word problem, this number follows the term "of".
- On the number side, the numerator is the number that's equal to the percent.

Examples:

How do you find the percentage when you know the number?

What is the number that is equal to 40% of 95?

$$\frac{\#}{} \quad \frac{\%}{}$$

$$\frac{x}{95} = \frac{40}{100}$$

Cross multiply:

$100(x) = 40(95)$

$100x = 3800$

$$\frac{100x}{100} = \frac{3800}{100}$$

$x = 38$

Answer: 38 is 40% of 95

How do you find the number when you know the percentage?

40% of what number is 38?

   #   %

$\dfrac{38}{x} = \dfrac{40}{100}$

Cross multiply:

100(38) = 40(x)

3800 = 40x

$\dfrac{3800}{40} = \dfrac{40x}{40}$

95 = x

Answer: 40% of 95 is 38

How do you find what percentage one number is of another?

What percentage of 95 is 38?

   #   %

$\dfrac{38}{95} = \dfrac{x}{100}$

Cross multiply:

100(38) = 95(x)

3800 = 95x

$\dfrac{3800}{95} = \dfrac{95x}{95}$

40 = x

Answer: 40% of 95 is 38

Calculating Rate

Calculating cost per unit, interest rate, and tax rate are common problems found on the real estate exam. The purpose of rate is to compare two amounts, using various units of measure.

Rate formula: $\dfrac{x \text{ units}}{y \text{ units}}$

Calculating cost per unit

Example:

How much do 2 square feet cost if 250 square feet cost $2,500?

Answer:

$\dfrac{2,500}{250}$ = $10 / square foot

Therefore, 2 square feet cost $20

Interest rate

The formula for simple interest is:

Interest = principal x rate x time

Basic Percentage

Determining basic percentage.

Example:

How do you calculate 53% of $3,645?

Answer:

Convert 53% to a decimal by moving the decimal two units to the left of the number.

53% = .53

Multiply the result by $3,645.

(.53) (3645) = $1,931.85

$1,931.85 is 53% of $3,645.

Percentage: Interest

How do you calculate the rate of interest being charged?

Example:

Paul Billings borrowed $22,000. He is paying $1,200 / year in interest. What is the interest rate he is being charged?

I = principal x rate x time

The principal amount is $22,000

The interest amount is $1,200

Rate = x

Time = 1 year

Using the formula, Interest = principal x rate x time, solve for x.

1,200 = 22,000(x)(1)

1,200 = 22,000x

$$\frac{1,200}{22,000} = \frac{x}{22,000}$$

.055 = x

Convert the decimal to a percent. Do this by moving the decimal two places to the right.

.055 = 5.5%

Area of Various Figures

Rectangles

Keep in mind: The formula for area in a rectangle is: Area = (length) (width)

Example:

Theresa purchased two small lots of land. One is 70 feet by 20 feet and the other, 80 feet by 30 feet. What is the total square feet of land that she has?

Answer:

A = (70) (20) + (80) (30) =

A = 1400 + 2400 = 3800 square feet

Theresa has a total of 3800 square feet in land.

How do you find the length of a rectangle if you only know the area and width?

Keep in mind: The formula for area in a rectangle is: Area = (length) (width)

Example:

Theresa has 2400 square feet of land that is 30 feet in width. What is the length of the land?

Answer:

2400 = (x) (30)

$\frac{2400}{30} = \frac{(x)(30)}{(30)}$

$x = \frac{2400}{30}$

x = 80 feet

Triangles

Keep in mind: The formula for area in a triangle is: Area = $\frac{1}{2}$ bh

Example:

For their small business, Paul and Sally Green are buying a triangular piece of land. The base of the property is 150 feet. The side that is perpendicular to the base is also 150 feet. What is the total number of square feet for the property?

Area = x

Base = 150

Height = 150

$x = (\frac{1}{2}$ or .5$)(150)(150)$

$x = (\frac{1}{2}$ or .5$)(22{,}500)$

x = 11,250 square feet

Circles

Keep in mind: The formula for area in a circle is: $A = \pi r^2$

Example:

Gill is using a circular prop on a circular piece of land for a special project. The radius of the circular land area is 23 feet. What is the area of the prop?

For "π", use 3.14.

What do you know?

Radius = 23

π = 3.14

Area = x

Solve.

$A = \pi r^2$

A = (3.14)(23)(23) = 1,661.06 square feet

The area of the prop is 1,661.06 square feet.

Property Tax

Property tax questions are solved using percents and rates.

Example:

Laurie Collins lives in Purple County. The tax rate for Purple County is $5.89 per hundred of assessed valuation. Ms. Collins shares that she pays $2,550 in taxes. What is her property assessment? Round answer to nearest 10 cents.

What do you know?

Taxes = $2,550

Tax rate = $5.89 per hundred (%)

Assessment = x

$5.89 is 5.89%. Convert the percentage to a decimal: .0589

.0589 of the assessed value of the house is $2,550, which means:

(.0589) (x) = 2,550

Solve.

$$\frac{.0589x}{.0589} = \frac{2,550}{.0589}$$

x = $43,293.718

Rounded to the nearest 10 cents, the answer is $43,293.70.

How do you determine the tax rate if you know the amount of taxes paid and assessment amount?

Example:

Mrs. Ferguson said her taxes are $1,300 and property assessment $40,000. What is the tax rate percentage?

What do you know?

Taxes = $1,300

Assessment = $40,000

Rate (%) = x

In equation form, this means:

($40,000) (x) = 1,300

Solve.

$$\frac{40,000x}{40,000} = \frac{1,300}{40,000}$$

x = .0325

Convert to a percentage.

The rate is 3.25%

Loan-to-Value Ratios (LTV)

Problems regarding Loan-to-Value Ratios typically involve percentages.

A mortgage loan for 25% is at an 85% LTV. The interest on the original balance for year #1 is $21,474. When securing the loan, what was the value of the property? Round to the nearest penny.

Solve.

Step #1: Determine the loan amount.

What do you know?

25% of the loan amount is $21,474.

Loan amount = x

In equation form this means:

($21,474) = (20%) (x) OR ($21,474) = (.2) (x)

$$\frac{21,474}{.2} = \frac{.2x}{.2}$$

x = $107,370

The loan amount is $107, 370

Step #2: Determine the value of the property.

What do you know?

Loan amount = $107,370

Loan-to-value ratio = 85%

Value = x

$107,370 is 85% of the value

In equation form this means:

(85% or .85) (x) = $107,370

$$\frac{.85x}{.85} = \frac{107,370}{.85}$$

x = 126,317.64

The value amount is $126,317.64

Points

"Point" is the term used to describe loan discounts. Each point represents a percentage of the face amount of the loan. For example, 3 points means 3% of the face amount of the loan.

Example:

Burt is attempting to obtain an $80,000 FHA mortgage loan. In order to do so, he must pay a 2-point discount (2%). What is the discount amount?

Answer:

Before solving the problem, convert the percentage to a decimal.

2% = .02

What do you know?

Amount of the loan = $80,000

Points = .02

Amount of the discount = x

x = (.02) (80,000)

x = $1,600

Equity

How do you calculate the value of a home?

Example:

John owns a home of which he has three mortgages. The first mortgage balance is $190,000. The second mortgage balance is $20,000 and third mortgage balance, $10,000. The equity in John's home is $50,000. What is the value of John's home?

In this problem, the value of the home is the total of all three mortgages plus the equity.

Answer:

$190,000 + $20,000 + $10,000 + $50,000 = $270,000

The value of the home is $270,000.

Qualifying Buyers

Megan is attempting to qualify for an FHA loan to buy a home. Her ratio requirement is 34/41. She makes $75,000 / year and has a $900 monthly car payment. What is her maximum PITI payment?

Answer:

First, divide Megan's annual income by the number of months in a year (12).

$75,000 ÷ 12 = $6,250

Megan's monthly income is $6,250

Next, determine the front-end qualifier by multiplying Megan's monthly income by the front-end portion (in decimal form) of the ratio.

$6,250 (.34) = $2,125

$2,125 is the front-end qualifier

Lastly, determine the back-end qualifier by multiplying Megan's monthly income by the back-end portion (in decimal form) of the ratio. Then subtract Megan's debt amount from this number.

$6,250 (.41) = $2,562.50 - $900 = $1,662.50

$1662.50 is the back-end qualifier

The maximum PITI is $1,662.50. PITI is the lower of the two qualifiers.

Prorations

During settlement, there is typically a reconciliation that needs to take place regarding money that is owed as of the settlement date. The best way to remember who owes what is by remembering the simple fact that he who uses the service is the one who has to pay for it. When calculating these figures, unless otherwise noted, you must always use a 30-day month and 360-day calendar year.

Example:

Mr. Perkins paid his 2012 property taxes in the amount of $2,400 one year in advance. He sells his house to Mr. Dickinson in April 2012 and settles in May of that same year. With regard to the amount paid in taxes, how much do the two gentlemen owe each other?

What do you know?

	Mr. Perkins	Mr. Dickinson
How many months paid for?	12 ($2,400)	0 ($0)
How many months used/will use?	4 ($800)	8 ($1,600)
How many months should he **be** reimbursed for?	8 ($1,600)	0 ($0)
How many months should he reimburse for?	0 ($1,600)	8 ($1,600)

Mr. Dickinson should be debited $1,600. Mr. Perkins should be credited $1,600.

Commissions

Commission calculation problems are common. They usually seek to determine a percentage, but they may also ask for a dollar amount.

Example:

The broker made her first home sale for $127,000. The total amount of commission is $7,700. What is the broker's commission rate?

Answer:

What do you know?

Home price: $127,000

Commission: $7,700

Commission rate: x

In equation form, this means:

127,000x = 7,700

Solve.

$$\frac{127,000x}{127,000} = \frac{7,700}{127,000}$$

x = 0.060

Change to a decimal and round to the nearest whole percent.

0.060 = 6%

Example:

An agent made a 6% commission on the sale of a home. The sale price was $345,867. The agent made another 6% commission on the sale of a $243,542 home. What is the total dollar amount the agent received in commission on the two homes?

Determine the commission amount on the first home sale.

$345,867 (.06) = $20,752.02

Determine the commission amount on the second home sale.

$243,542 (.06) = $14,612.52

Add together the two commission amounts.

$20,752.02 + $14,612.52 = $35,364.54

Total commission = $35,364.54

Sale Proceeds

Example:

The agent is working with the homeowner to determine the list price for the homeowner's home in order to meet the homeowner's desire to at least net $30,000. The current mortgage balance is $235,000 and commission to take into consideration is 7%. If they list and sell the property at $300,000, will the homeowner net at least $30,000?

What do you know?

Expenses: Total - $256,000

       Mortgage balance: $235,000

       Commission: $21,000

Sale price: $300,000

$235,000 + $21,000 = $256,000

$300,000 - $256,000 = $44,000

The homeowner will net $44,000. Therefore, he will net at least $30,000.

Transfer Tax/Conveyance Tax/Revenue Stamps

Transfer tax is **not** used in the state of Indiana, but it is used in some other states.

For example:

The Massachusetts Tax Stamp in most counties is $4.56 / $1000 of the home's sale price.

Transfer Tax (Massachusetts Tax Stamp) Example:

A homeowner sells her house for $432,000. How much does she owe the state for tax stamps?

There are 432 ($1,000s) in $432,000. Therefore, you multiply the stamp amount per $1,000, which is $4.56 times 432.

$4.56 x 432 = $1,969.92

The tax stamp amount for the sale of a $432,000 home is $1,969.92.

Transfer Tax (Massachusetts Tax Stamp) Example:

A homeowner sells his property for $297,765. The tax stamp is $1,357.81. If the tax stamp is calculated per $1,000 of the sale price, what is the rate (per $1,000) of the tax stamp?

Answer:

What do you know?

Sale price: $297,765

Tax stamp: x per $1,000

Tax stamp amount: $1,357.83

Solve.

$$\frac{\$297,765}{\$1,000} = \$297.77$$

$1,357.83 = (x)($297.77)

$$\frac{\$1,357.83}{\$297.77} = \frac{(x)(\$297.77)}{(\$297.77)}$$

4.56 = x

The tax stamp rate is $4.56 per $1000.

Competitive Market Analyses (CMA)

CMAs help sellers get a better understanding of the market value of their property, which could in turn help them decide on the sale price. Although very useful, it is important to note that CMAs are not appraisals.

CMA problems are solved by using measurable aspects of comparable properties to come to a specific value.

Example:

Mr. Stone has the blueprint for two homes he would like to build. Home A is 62' x 94' in size and will cost $234,985 to build. Home B is 90' x 112' in size. If each house costs the same per square foot to build, how much will it cost to build Home B?

Answer:

Remember, the formula to find Area for a rectangle is: A = lw.

Area of Home A: 62(94) = 5,828 square feet

Area of Home B: 90(112) = 10,080 square feet

Cost to build Home A / square foot: $\frac{\$234,985}{5,828}$ = $40.32

Cost to build Home B = 10,080($40.32) = $406,425.60

Income Properties

Example:

Bob, a local real estate investor is interested in buying an income property that creates gross income in the amount of $270,500. He discovers that the operating costs of this property will equal 65% of the gross income. Ideally, he would like to acquire a 15% return. With his desire to have a 15% return, what is the most he can pay for the property?

Answer:

What do you know?

Gross income= $270,500

Operating costs= 65% of $270,500

Net income = Gross income – operating costs

Desired return= 15%

Most the investor can pay = x

Step #1:

Determine the dollar amount of the operating costs. Start off by converting the percentage to a decimal.

65% = .65

Operating costs = (.65)(270,500) = $175,825

Step #2:

Gross income – Operating costs = Net income

$270,500 - $175,825 = $94,675

Step #3:

The investor wants his net income to be 15% of what he pays for the property. Convert the percent to a decimal, and then determine the most he can pay.

15% = .15

$94,675 = (.15)(x)

$$\frac{\$94{,}675}{.15} = \frac{(.15)(x)}{.15}$$

$$\frac{\$94{,}675}{.15} = x$$

$631,167 (Rounded to the nearest dollar)

Depreciation

You may encounter "depreciation" problems on the exam, but those representing the straight-line method are the only ones you will probably see.

The formula for the straight-line method of depreciation:

$$\frac{replacement\ cost}{years\ of\ useful\ life} = annual\ depreciation$$

If the depreciation rate is not given, you can calculate it dividing the total depreciation, which is 100%, by the useful life of the building.

For example, if a building has 25 years of useful life, then you will use this calculation:

$$\frac{100\%}{25} = 4\%$$

This means that the building has an annual depreciation rate of 4%.

Example:

It has been determined that the replacement cost of a 15 year old building is $90,000. Since it has 35 years of useful life left, how much can be charged to annual depreciation?

What do you know?

Replacement cost = $90,000

Useful life = 35 years

Using the formula $\frac{replacement\ cost}{years\ of\ useful\ life}$ = annual depreciation, calculate annual depreciation.

$$\frac{\$90,000}{35} = \$2571 \text{ (Rounded to the nearest dollar)}$$

Example:

The annual depreciation of a building is $3245. What is the total depreciation of a 19 year old building?

annual depreciation x age of building = total depreciation

$3245 x 19 = $61,655

Total depreciation = $61,655

Example:

The replacement cost of a building is $62,000. The total depreciation of said building is $19,354. What is the current value of the building?

replacement cost – depreciation = current value

$62,000 - $19,354 = $42,646

Current value of the building = $42,646

Summary

It is our hope that this Real Estate Math review has helped reinforce your knowledge of the topics you will most likely see on the math section of the Real Estate Exam. For those of you who feel like you could use a bit more of a refresher, feel free to take the included practice exams over and over until you feel confident that you can triumphantly complete the Real Estate Exam. Good luck!

Real Estate Glossary

>A

abandonment giving up the right to possess a property, building or real estate area through non-use and intention.
abstract of title the background of a property listing legal transactions and information.
abutting sitting next to another property.
acceleration clause an addendum that forces the borrower to repay the entire loan upon the lender's insistence for specific reasons listed in the clause.
acceptance agreement to an offer.
accretion increase of the amount of land by natural deposits of soil on onto the property.
accrued depreciation the total loss of value on the property.
accrued items the additional costs still outstanding at the close of the real estate deal, such as interest, insurance, HOA   fees or taxes.
acknowledgement agreement to fulfill admitted responsibility.
acre a section of land that is 4,840 square yards or 43,560 square feet in area.
actual eviction a step-by-step procedure to remove renters from property.
actual notice specific information given to a party, such as a tenant, landlord, buyer or seller.
addendum a clause that provides more specific information to clarify a contract.
adjacent property or buildings next to each other but might not touch each other.
adjoining property or buildings next to each other that do touch each other.

adjustable rate mortgage a loan rate that changes throughout the period of the loan. Sometimes called a variable rate or flexible rate.
adjusted basis the final cost of a property after improvements are added and deductions or reduced value are subtracted.
adjustment date the date agreed upon by the buyer and seller for financial changes.
administrator a court-appointed individual who executes a person's estate if there is not a will.
ad valorem tax property tax on the current value of the land.
adverse possession The ways by which a person may acquire property, such as through purchase, inheritance or other methods, including without payment as in a squatter.
affidavit a sworn promise before a person in authority.
agency a professional company who can act on behalf of another, such as a real estate agency or a title agency.
agent a professional individual who can act on behalf of another, such as a real estate agent or a title agent.
agreement of sale a contract between two parties to buy/sell property, usually over time.
air rights the right to air space above a property, separate from the property land itself.
alienation placement of ownership of property from one person/company to another person/company.
alienation clause an addendum to the mortgage contract that keeps the borrower from reselling the property without paying the lender.
allodial system a national system overseen by law that monitors property ownership.
amenities "extras" on a property that make it worth more or more attractive to buyers. Location or kitchen upgrades are two examples of amenities.
amortization paying off the principle and interest on a debt with equal payments until the debt is repaid.
amortization schedule the time frame set up over which the principle and interest of the debt is repaid.
amortize to pay off the principle and interest on a loan.
annual percentage rate (APR) the percentage above the principle added onto the loan over 12 months. It includes additional costs, such as closing costs and fees, and not just interest rates.
anti-deficiency law a statute that stops the lender from pursuing the buyer for a loss on a property after a foreclosure sale.
anti-trust laws national laws that encourage free market trade and practices and prohibit the restriction of such.
apportionments the division of costs, such as fees and HOA responsibilities, between the seller and purchaser.
appraisal assessing the worth of land or property by a professional, qualified person who is usually licensed.
appraised value the worth of the land or property as determined by the licensed professional.
appraiser a professional, qualified person so licensed by the state to determine the value of land or property.
appreciation growth in the worth of real estate.
appurtenance an attachment to land or edifices that now conveys with the property.
arbitration dispute resolution through the use of a third party.

ARELLO an online company that encourages the cooperation of decision makers in the real estate business.
assessed value the tax-related value put on a property.
assessment the placement of tax-related value on a property.
assessor a professional who determines the tax-related value of a property.
asset something of value that belongs to a person, such as cash, property, bonds, etc.
assignment the transfer of a mortgage from one agency to another.
assumption the process of the buyer taking over the seller's mortgage.
attachment placing a legal hold on a property to pay for a judgment.
attest to agree to the truth of a document by signing it.
attorney-in-fact a person who acts as a legal representative for another; does not need to be a professional lawyer.
avulsion transfer of land because water, such as a stream or brook, changes course.

>B

balloon mortgage a mortgage with small payments due for a specified period, such as three to five years with a lump sum or balloon due at the end of the mortgage.
balloon payment the lump payment at the end of a balloon mortgage.
bankruptcy the legal discharge of most debts through the courts.
bargain and sale deed a document transferring property from seller to buyer without guaranteeing the validity of the transfer.
baseline a line in surveying that runs east to west and acts a point of reference for corresponding lines that run north to south.
benchmark a fixed point of reference by which elevation is marked.
beneficiary the recipient of the profits that occur as a result of someone else's actions
bequest similar to an inheritance, a transfer of personal property through a will.
betterment an upgrade to property.
bilateral contract a contract, such as a rent agreement, when both parties agree to comply with or not comply with certain terms.
bill of sale a legal paper that transfers ownership of property from one person (company) to another.
binder money paid to hold a property for set terms.
biweekly mortgage payments made on real estate every two weeks as opposed to once a month. In some cases, this reduces the time needed to pay off the loan.
blanket mortgage a mortgage owned by the same person on at least two properties.
blockbusting an illegal process that involves scaring residents of an area into selling their property at reduced prices so that an agent can take advantage them.
bona fide legal adjective that describes faithful, trustworthy actions or people.
bond a type of insurance money that protects a professional against loss.
boot a sum of cash included in a buyer/seller agreement to even out exchange.
branch office a satellite or another office that is at separate place from headquarters, for example, the headquarters is in Indianapolis with branch offices in Bloomington, South Bend, and Marion.

breach of contract breaking a binding agreement illegally.
broker professional or entity that is qualified through classes and licensed to buy or sell property.
brokerage a firm that employs one or more real estate professionals; real estate company.
broker's price opinion (BPO) an estimate on the worth of real estate by a professional in the industry.
building code state and local legislation that regulates new edifices or structural changes or existing ones.
building line an invisible boundary line around the property. The building must stay within this boundary.
building restrictions state, local and neighborhood guidelines or constraints that guide how it is built or determine property use.
bundle of rights privileges associated with property ownership, such as residency or use.
buy down payment by the buyer of added fees or points to the seller or lender for a lower interest rate.
buyer's broker a real estate professional who searches for a property and conducts negotiations in order to purchase the property.
bylaws procedural guidelines used to conduct business or meetings at an organization like a homeowner's association.

>C

cancellation clause a section in a contract that permits parties to nullify the obligations of the contract.
canvassing surveying or soliciting an area to see if people are interested in selling their home.
cap the maximum increase in interest for a mortgage with changing rates.
capital funds used to generate more money.
capital expenditure money spent to improve the value of real estate.
capital gains tax taxation on the proceeds from a property sale.
capitalization the total yearly potential earnings on a property, such as a rental.
capitalization rate a percentage that can be used to compare investment opportunities. This is determined by dividing   the yearly capitalization by the cost of the property.
cash flow the final amount of income generated from a rental property after income and expenses.
caveat emptor Latin expression meaning "let the buyer beware." Serves as a warning to the buyer.
CC&R covenants, conditions and restrictions – The bylaws for a group of homeowners.
certificate of discharge an IRS document that enables the government to waive taxes on a property.
certificate of eligibility formal document from the Veteran's Administration that proves the person qualifies for a VA loan.
certificate of reasonable value (CRV) the maximum value permitted for a VA mortgage.
certificate of sale permits the buyer to receive the title for the purchase of the property.

certificate of title an official decision on the ownership, status or availability of a piece of real estate through public documents.
chain of title the legal document that tells the history of a piece of real estate.
chattel any property someone owns except real estate.
chattel mortgage the use of personal property as security for debt repayment.
city an incorporate group of residences larger than a town or village.
clear title a document of ownership that is completely valid.
closing the final legal transfer of property ownership through the signing of official papers.
closing costs the monies associated with the sale of property, such as inspection fees.
closing date the actual date the property will transfer from the buyer to the seller.
closing statement a final summary of all costs involved in the sale of real estate.
cloud on the title a questionable title as to the availability for sale.
clustering a group of residential buildings used to maximize land use.
codicil an addendum to a will that explains additions or deletions to the document.
coinsurance clause a clause in an insurance policy that divides financial responsibility for a loss between at least two parties.
collateral something of value that promises the repayment of a loan.
collection efforts to acquire delinquent rent or mortgage payments.
color of title a title that is invalid although it seemed to be valid initially.
commercial property real estate set aside for business use.
commingling combining the funds of two parties into one account
commission the payment that a broker or real estate agent receives for the sale of a property, usually a percentage of the sale price.
commitment letter a document from the mortgage company that informs the borrower regarding loan approval and the terms of said approval.
common areas regions of a neighborhood or apartment complex that all residents share, such as a pool, playground or parking lot.
common law originating in England, law based in part on traditions and in part on the courts.
community property real estate and chattel shared by 2 parties, usually husband and wife.
Comparable sales: Homes in the area that interested parties can assess to determine the worth of a piece of real estate.
comparative market analysis (CMA) assessing the worth of real estate through the value of similar pieces of real estate in the area.
competent parties someone who can legally sign a contract.
competitive market analysis (CMA) a list of benefits of the property and a comparison to other homes in the area. **condemnation** taking over ownership of a property, usually by the government, and paying the owner for the real estate.
condominium similar to apartments, individual residences in a building or area with common areas shared jointly by all residents.
condominium conversion the transfer in ownership in a condominium from one owner to many for each residence.
conformity the belief that similar pieces of real estate will retain their worth.
consideration a legal enticement that attracts the buyer to sign the contract.

construction mortgage a two-part loan – first, to pay for construction costs and next to pay for the home. Usually the borrower pays interest only payments until the home is finished when the mortgage transitions into a regular loan.
constructive eviction when a tenant moves out of a residence because of the poor quality of the residence without being liable for rent.
constructive notice public record and therefore common information to all.
contingency certain requirements that must be met to fulfill the contract, such as sale of the buyer's home so that he can afford the new residence
contract a legal arrangement between two legal parties that establishes certain conditions that will happen.
contract for deed a deferment of the price of the property for a specific time frame.
conventional loan financing to obtain a piece of property or real estate.
conversion option an agreement that the buyer can change an adjustable interest rate to a fixed rate. There is a cost associated with this option.
convertible ARM an agreement that the buyer can change an adjustable interest rate to a fixed rate. There is a cost associated with this option.
conveyance the legal transfer of property from one party to another.
cooperative ownership in shares of a common residential building, similar to an apartment, which allows the owners to live there.
corporation a company acts as its own business with liability and management.
cost approach a way to assess real estate value by starting with the worth of the property, subtracting costs and adding improvements.
counteroffer saying no to a real estate offer and then suggesting a different offer.
covenant specifications included in the deed requiring obligations or restrictions on real estate use.
covenant of seisin a legal verification that the owner has the right to the property.
credit available financial backing for real estate that needs to be repaid in the future.
credit history a list of borrowers or lenders who have lent the individual money and a history of how they have fulfilled their financial obligations.
cul-de-sac a semi-private road with a circular type of dead-end at the end, usually adds value in real estate.
curtesy a man's ownership of some or all of his spouse's property even if she will deny him such ownership.
cartilage the area in close proximity to a residence, including other buildings, but not including open lands away from the home.

>D

damages financial or other compensation to the hurt party for tangible or intangible losses.
datum a horizontal reference point used to make vertical measurements.
DBA "doing business as" – sometimes used as an "also known as" name for a company.
debt money or property that is owed to another and must be repaid.
debt service repayment over a specific time frame, usually of a mortgage, including interest and principal.

decedent a person who passed way, often used to discuss their estate, will, inheritance or other financial matters.
dedication a gift of property for the benefit of all and the receipt of land by authorities.
deed the official, written proof that transfers and verifies property ownership.
deed-in-lieu used instead of a foreclosure, the property owner returns the property deed back to the lender to avoid a public record of foreclosure in some cases.
deed of trust a type of mortgage used in some jurisdictions.
deed restriction part of the deed that prevents the owner from certain land uses.
default failure to make a loan payment within a certain time frame, usually within 30 days of the due date.
defeasance clause the legal option that the lender has to repossess delinquent payments or the property from the borrower in case of a default.
deficiency judgment a legal document ordering the collection of the difference between what a borrower owes to the bank and the sale price of a home.
delinquency late payment on a loan.
density zoning regulations that prohibit more than a certain number of homes in an area.
depreciation a reduction in the value of an asset because of financial, physical or use.
descent the passing down of property to an heir if the deceased person has not left specific provisions.
devise a gift of real estate to an heir through a will.
devisee the person who receives a gift of property from a will.
devisor the person who gives a gift of property to another through a will.
directional growth the direction in which a city is expanding.
discount point money paid to the mortgage holder to reduce the interest payment. The more money that is paid, the lower the interest will fall.
discount rate the interest rate that a bank will pay to the Federal Reserve to borrow cash for short-term loans.
dispossess legal process of eviction.
dominant estate (tenement) property that benefits from the shared use of land on a neighboring property.
dower a woman's ownership of some or all of her spouse's property even if his will denies her such ownership.
down payment cash, as part of the cost of real estate, paid separately from the financing.
dual agency a real estate agent or broker who acts on behalf of two or more parties in a sale.
due-on-sale clause the clause that requires the loan to be repaid to the lender when the real estate is sold.
duress a person feels threatened into doing something, such as selling property.

>E

earnest money money to prove the buyer's serious intent of purchasing the home.
easement an agreement that one person has the privilege of use of another's land.
easement by necessity the need to walk on someone else's property by necessity.

easement by prescription accepted use of property by another person that is unnecessary. This becomes legal when it occurs over a certain number of years, such as a short cut through a neighbor's yard.
easement in gross accepted use of property that remains with the individual and does not convey with the property. For example, when the home is sold to a different owner, the easements are not passed to the new owner.
economic life the length of time when real estate will continue to earn money.
effective age the age of the building based on the condition of the building.
emblements different types of farming crops considered part of property.
eminent domain the purchase of private property by the government for public purposes.
encroachment part of real estate that crosses property boundaries onto another's property.
encumbrance assessments against a property, such as delinquent HOA fees, any mortgages or easements that impact the value.
equitable title the right someone who has to a property when they commit to buy it although the deal is not yet finalized.
equity the worth of the property above the mortgage or other debts on the property.
equity of redemption the reclaiming of real estate by the mortgage holder because of foreclosure.
erosion slow wearing away of land by natural elements, such as flooding.
escalation clause passing on increased expenses to tenants, such as fuel or HOA fees.
escheat real estate goes to the state if a person dies without a will and without any heirs.
escrow money or something of value held in trust by a third party until the completion of a specific transaction.
escrow account monies collected from the buyer that the lender holds in reserve to pay property taxes and homeowner's insurance.
escrow analysis a yearly review that assesses the monies collected in escrow to ensure that the amount is correct. It may be increased or decreased at that time to reconcile the account.
escrow disbursements the use of the escrow account to pay taxes, insurances and expenses.
estate all of a person's property.
estate for years time frame during which a person accesses land or property.
estate tax the tax on the worth of the assets when a person dies. A certain portion of the estate is exempt.
estoppel certificate written confirmation that the borrower signs stating that the mortgage amount is correct.
et al. Latin for "and others;" used to refer to property ownership by several people, "Jane Doe, et. al."
et ux. Latin for "and wife".
et vir. Latin for "and husband".
eviction the process by which a person is legally removed from a property.
evidence of title official paperwork that proves that someone own the property.
examination of title history of the title although not as complete or detailed as a title search.
exchange similar business or investment properties that can be traded tax-free per IRS Code 1031.

exclusive agency listing a binding legal agreement that gives a single broker permission to sell real estate for a certain time frame.

exclusive right to sell a binding legal agreement that gives the real estate agent the right to collect the commission if anyone else sells the property during the specified time frame.

exculpatory clause permits the borrower to give back the real estate to the lien holder without personal responsibility to repay the mortgage.

execution when a creditor wants to enforce the payment of the debt, they will require the debtor to turn over the property.

executor/executrix the person established by the deceased to perform estate duties. Executrix is a female who performs these duties.

executory contract a legal agreement that is awaiting action by at least one party for completion.

executed contract a completed contract.

express contract a contract that details all aspects of the contract, such as offer, acceptance and consideration.

extension agreement a mutual decision to lengthen the time frame for a contract.

external obsolescence a reduction in the worth of a specific home improvement because of something separate from the real estate that decreases the worth of the home.

> F

fair housing law a national statute that prohibits discrimination in any housing dealings because of race, color, sex, religion, family status, handicap or national origin.

fair market value what the property will sell for according to both a buyer and seller.

Federal Housing Administration (FHA) a government agency that guarantees loans to make housing easier to obtain.

Federal National Mortgage Association (Fannie Mae) a federal organization that helps keep the home loan market solvent by purchasing notes from bankers.

Federal Reserve System the government banking system that oversees banks, offers services and sets national economic policy.

fee simple full and complete ownership of real estate.

FHA-insured loan a mortgage that is backed by the government through the FHA. VA loans are also backed by the government.

fiduciary relationship a person who acts on another's behalf in business or general matters.

finder's fee money that the realtor pays to a third party who finds a buyer; usually illegal.

first mortgage the first loan taken out on a home, usually in chronological order, but not always.

fixed-rate loan a loan where the interest rate remains the same throughout the loan term.

fixture personal property affixed to the building that conveys with the building when it is sold.

foreclosure the process by which a buyer loses the property because of failure to pay the debt, which result s in the public sale of the real estate in order to pay as much of the debt as possible.

forfeiture seizure of property because of criminal actions or failure to fulfill a contract.

franchise when a business owner pays to use a company name in return for company backing, such as member brokerages.
fraud deceptive actions intended to mislead another person and harm them
freehold estate continued ownership or stake in a property as compared to a temporary stake or a lease.
front foot the measurement at the front of the home nearest the street; used to compare home value especially on the same street
functional obsolescence the decrease in worth on the real estate except those caused by wear and tear
future interest a right to real estate that will come to pass in the future.

>G

general agent someone who can do any job duties related to the business on behalf of the principal. A real estate agent acts as a special agent.
general lien a mortgage that covers more than one property owned by the same person.
general warranty deed a guarantee that the title is free and clear of other claims against it for the protection of the buyer.
government-backed mortgage a loan that is backed by the federal government as contrasted with a conventional loan.
Government National Mortgage Association (Ginnie Mae) a federal agency that supplies funding for government loans.
government survey system a process of dividing land into rectangle sections in order to set area boundaries.
graduated lease a rental agreement that permits periodic adjustments in rental price increases.
grant the exchanging of real estate to another individual through a deed.
grant deed the legal document used to transfer real estate to another.
grantee the person who receives the real estate; buyer.
grantor the person who sells the real estate.
gross income all financial gains received for real estate before any losses or expenses on the property.
gross income multiplier a way to assess the profitability of property arrived at by dividing the total price paid by the monthly rental rate.
gross lease a rental agreement when the landlord pays all costs associated with the property, including HOA fees, repairs, taxes and more.
gross rent multiplier a way to assess the profitability of property arrived at by dividing the total price paid by the monthly rental rate
ground lease a lease of land only, not of buildings.
guaranteed sale plan a contract between the seller and the real estate agent/broker. The broker promises to buy the property for predetermined terms if the property does not sell by a certain date.
guardian a person who the court deems legally responsible for someone who is incapable of managing their affairs.

>H

Habendum clause "To have and to hold" that specifies any restrictions on property; fee simple absolute.
hamlet a small, populated area; municipality.
heir someone who receives property, often through a will after a death.
hereditament anything either tangible or intangible given through a will.
highest and best use the most productive use of real estate that will provide the greatest financial return over a specified period of time.
holdover tenancy a renter who stays on the property when the lease ends.
Holographic will a handwritten will signed by the person who makes the will; does not need a notary or witness.
home equity conversion mortgage (HECM) Reverse mortgage or when a lender makes payments, usually monthly, to a homeowner.
home equity line of credit a loan available to homeowners based on the equity in the home, similar to a credit card.
home inspection a professional assessment of the real estate that closely examines the property.
homeowner's insurance an insurance policy that covers the property and contents against all types of natural and other damages, includes liability.
homeowner's warranty insurance coverage that protects the buyer against any defects in the residence.
homestead permitted by some states, protects a residence against lawsuits or judgments up to certain limits.
HUD Housing Urban and Development Department, federal agency that regulates some aspects of the housing industry.
hypothecate a promise of something as pledge for a loan without physically relinquishing that item. Most home owners live in their primary residence through this method unless they own the residence free and clear.

>I

implied contract an informal contract, not in writing, yet enforceable by the courts.
improvement work done on land or property that increases worth, additions or upgrades that are more consequential than repairs.
income capitalization approach a specific formula used to assess the income-producing worth of a property.
income property real estate that earns money for the owner.
incorporeal right intangible rights associated with real estates, such as easements and future income.
indemnify to insure against loss.
independent contractor the employment status of most real estate agents; those who work independently and do not have an employer/employee relationship.

index an assessment of the current financial atmosphere by the government; used to adjust prices.
industrial property real estate used for non-residential but business purposes, such as a warehouse or manufacturing property.
inflation an increase in overall costs and expenses that results in a decrease in what money will buy.
initial interest rate the first or starting rate for an adjustable mortgage.
installment a scheduled payment toward the reduction of debt, such as a mortgage.
installment contract a binding, legal, written agreement that sets a schedule for the loan payments.
installment loan a loan that is repaid in periodic payments at a set schedule; sometimes secured by personal property.
installment sale payments made to a seller over a longer period of time in order to defer taxes.
insurance money paid to an indemnity holder to reduce the expenses associated with the specific emergency being insured, such as flooding or earthquakes.
insurance binder temporary proof of insurance until the permanent paperwork is completed.
insured mortgage financial backing for a loan that protects the lender against default, sometimes called PMI.
interest a legal right to real estate or other property; B. The amount a lender charges a borrower for the loan above the principal, usually specified as a percentage.
interest accrual rate how often the interest accrues, such as daily, weekly or monthly, until it is paid to the lender.
interest rate the amount a lender charges a borrower for the loan above the principle, usually specified as a percentage.
interest rate buydown plan a plan that uses money from a still uncompleted home sale to reduce the interest rate and the monthly costs to the buyer.
interest rate ceiling the maximum percentage rate cap on an adjustable rate mortgage.
interest rate floor the lowest percentage rate minimum on an adjustable rate mortgage.
interim financing a transitional loan to bridge the time frame until the buyer can obtain permanent financing, for example a construction loan.
intestate without a legal will or without any will at all.
invalid not legally enforceable, such as a will or a contract.
investment property real estate purchased for the purpose of generating income.

>J

joint tenancy more than one individual who owns property in common, usually related individuals.
joint venture more than one entity who works toward the same professional goal, usually a temporary arrangement for a specific purpose.
judgment the court order that sets the amount one person or entity owes another in the event of a default, such as a loan or in an eviction.
judgment lien a lender's right to claim the property of the borrower because of a judgment.

judicial foreclosure court order to force the sale of real estate to pay off debt. The satisfaction of debts will stop foreclosure.
jumbo loan a property loan above the normal limits.
junior mortgage a loan that will only be satisfied after the first mortgage.

>L

laches the delay of the time period during which a legal claim can be enforced.
land solid real estate, separate from water or air.
landlocked property that is not accessible to public roads except through a neighboring property.
lease a legal contact that lasts for a specific time period during which the owner allows the renter to possess the property.
leased fee a restriction on property because of a rental/lease agreement.
lease option the renter can decide to buy the property under certain conditions.
leasehold property subject to a long-term rental agreement.
legal description authoritative confirmation of a property through written, technical means.
lessee tenant of real estate property.
lessor landlord of real estate property.
leverage the mortgage used to purchase a home or business.
levy a legal order of payment of any money due.
license legal permission, such as the temporary use of property.
lien financial assessment against real estate that must be paid when the land is sold.
life estate a lifelong interest in a specific real estate that ends when the owner dies.
life tenant someone who can stay on the real estate property until their death.
liquidity the availability of cash when using assets, such as property or real estate.
lis pendens Latin for "suit pending." Notice of possible restrictions on title when a lawsuit is filed.
listing agreement a contract between a real estate agent and client that pays commission to the agent no matter how the buyer finds the property.
listing broker the real estate agent who lists the property.
littoral rights the shore land next to an ocean or very large water body that the property owner has rights to.
loan borrowing money from another entity.
loan officer a representative for the lender or a representative for the borrower to the lender who may also look for loans.
lock-in the borrower pays a fee to guarantee a certain interest rate for a specific time period, especially if the borrower thinks the interest rates will rise.
lock-in period the time frame of the lock-in, such as 90 days.
lot and block description a legal process of finding real estate based on its lot and block identification within the housing area.

>M

management agreement a legal agreement between an owner and a property manager for a percentage of the rental generated.
margin a flat percentage to adjust interest rates up or down according to the index used in adjustable rate mortgages.
market data approach a comparison of recent property sales to assess real estate worth.
market value in real estate, price range between the maximum purchase price and minimum purchase price.
marketable title a free-and-clear title.
mechanic's lien a hold on the construction and on the real estate that guarantees payment for the work done on the property.
metes and bounds specific description of the land that identifies all boundaries of the real estate.
mill one-tenth of a penny; used for taxation.
minor a person who is not of legal age to make a binding decision.
misrepresentation a misleading verbalization even if unintended.
modification a legal alteration to a contract.
money judgment a court order that orders a financial payment.
month-to-month tenancy a rental agreement that can be extended or cancelled each month.
monument a landmark or immovable object used to decide the land locations.
mortgage a loan on property that uses the property itself as security for the repayment of the property.
mortgage banker a bank that finances loans for others, which are then sometimes purchased by federal agencies.
mortgage broker an agency that researches and finds loans for others but does not finance them.
mortgage lien the financing on a piece of real estate that obligates the buyer to the holder.
mortgagee the person/agency who lends money in a real estate transaction
mortgagor the person/agency who borrows money in a real estate transaction.
multi-dwelling units a building, such as an apartment complex, that has separate living units but only one property loan.
multiple-listing system (MLS- also multiple-listing service) a group of real estate agents that lists all the available properties for sale, which gives a buyer a wide range of choices.
mutual rescission an agreement to void a contract by all involved parties.

>N

negative amortization a deferment of interest payments on a loan, which is added on to the principal and results in an eventual increase in the payments over time and a loss of value on the home.
net income when all bills have been paid, the earnings that remain.
net lease the renter, as opposed to the landlord, pays costs, such as HOA fees, repairs and upkeep.
net listing any funds above the original price of the property that are paid to the real estate agent, illegal in some places.

net worth the positive, monetary difference between the value of assets and liabilities.
no cash-out refinance sometimes called a "rate and term refinance," the borrower receives no cash, but the money is used to recalculate the loan and related costs.
non-conforming use a code violation related to property use that is permitted because it was "grandfathered in." In   other words, the property owner began the questionable property use before the zoning ordinance took effect.
nonliquid asset something of worth that is difficult to convert to cash.
notarize to witness the veracity of a signature.
notary public a person with the legal and official authority to witness the veracity of a signature.
note the written loan that admits debt and promises repayment.
note rate the interest rate on a loan or mortgage.
notice of default official notification that the borrower has defaulted and that the lender can take additional legal   remedies.
novation the substitution of one party for another party in a contract.

>O

obligee a person requesting a certain duty in their favor.
obligor a person required to perform a certain duty, often under bond.
obsolescence a decrease in worth because of outdated design or construction, such as a home without a dishwasher or cable hook-up.
offer a suggestion or expression of desire to buy or sell real estate.
offer and acceptance the suggestion or expression of desire to buy or sell real estate and the acceptance of the offer by the other party.
open-end mortgage a loan with smaller amount than the maximum funds that a borrower can access from the lender.
open listing more than one real estate agent can list the property; the first to close the sale is the one who receives payment .
opinion of title legal authentication that the title is clear.
option an agreement that allows a buyer to purchase a property at a specific price if done so within a specific time period.
optionee the person who has available choices.
optionor the person who gives or sells the available choices.
ordinance a statute or legislations related to property use.
original principal balance the loan amount before the first payment is made.
origination fee fees assessed to the borrower that cover loan expenses related to the title, appraisal and credit checks.
owner financing the seller provides the buyer with the loan; the buyer does not go through a bank.
ownership possession of property.

>P
package mortgage a combination loan that covers both the residence and the land.

parcel a section of real estate under the person who owns it.
participation mortgage a loan that permits the holder to receive a portion of the profits from the property.
partition equal division of property between all owners.
partnership business relationship between 2 or more parties subject to debt and tax laws.
party wall a wall that divides 2 properties with ownership rights for both users.
payee the seller who receives money or something of value.
payor the buyer who gives the payee money or something of value.
percentage lease a rental payment determined by sales volume of the renter with a minimum rental amount.
periodic estate a rental agreement that goes for a specific time frame, such as month-to-month.
personal property (hereditaments) anything either tangible or intangible given through a will.
physical deterioration decrease in property worth because of normal wear, failure to repair or things breaking .
PITI principal, interest, taxes and insurance payment; usually the total of all payments due on the property.
planned unit development (PUD) zoning permission to design a subdivision with flexibility and creativity .
plat description of a section of land that provides detailed information about the area.
plat book public information with the description of a section of land that provides detailed information about the area.
plat number the number associated with each lot in a plat.
plottage combining small sections of real estate into a larger parcel.
PMI private mortgage insurance; used to cover the default of the loan.
point one percent of the loan amount; monies paid to entice a lender to loan money to the borrower, sometimes used in exchange for a reduction in the interest rate on the loan.
point of beginning the exact same starting and ending point on a land survey as the survey borders and encloses the property.
police power the government's ability to address the overall well-being of the community.
power of attorney the legal right for one person to perform duties for another either some or all of the time.
preapproval qualifying a buyer prior to actual purchase of the home.
prepayment paying costs or monies due early, sometimes as escrow funds.
prepayment penalty the expenses associated with early pay-off of a loan.
prequalification preapproval, sometimes in writing, before the buyer can purchase the home.
prescription receiving the right to a property through common use, such as a squatter, or adverse possession.
primary mortgage market the original buyer of a loan, such as a bank or savings and loan, which may then be sold on   the secondary mortgage market for a profit.
prime rate the lowest available interest rate a lending institution charges on short-term loans to businesses.
principal the face value of a loan or mortgage, separate from the interest, taxes and insurance.

principal meridian an imaginary north/south line used as a reference point in surveying to describe land.
probate to confirm the authenticity of a will.
procuring cause a method of deciding if the real estate agent earned a commission, legal expression that means the goal was realized through the actions.
promissory note a written statement of a promise to pay.
property management oversight of different aspects of property, such as collecting payments, upkeep, leasing units, cleaning units.
property tax real estate tax based on worth that is collected by the government.
prorate to equally divide a financial assessment between a buyer and a seller, for example as HOA fees or property taxes.
pur autre vie "For the life of another;" use of property that one individual gives another, as long as the third person is alive.
purchase agreement also called contract of sale or agreement of sale; a written contract between a buyer and seller.
purchase money mortgage a mortgage loan that the purchaser gives the seller as partial payment for property.

>Q

qualifying ratios the ratio of the buyer's debt when compared to the buyer's income, which must be below a certain percentage for a lending institution to offer the loan.
quitclaim deed a release of rights in a property without confirming the validity or the rights of the person who keeps the deed.

>R

range A six mile wide area of land. Using the rectangular survey system, it is numbered East or West.
ready, willing, and able a buyer who is ready to buy and follows through with the requirements needed to close the sale.
real estate land, the air above it, the ground under it and any buildings.
real estate agent a person who acts on the behalf of another to make a transaction with a third party.
real estate board a group of professional agents who belong to the National Association of Realtors.
real estate broker a person who acts on the behalf of another to make a transaction with a third party.
Real Estate Settlement Procedures Act (RESPA) a law that informs buyers of their rights by requiring the lender to give updated information to the borrower throughout the home buying process.
real property real estate; physical land and structures on the land.
REALTOR a professional real estate agent.

recording the official documentation related to a change in property title, such as a sale or transfer.
rectangular survey system a survey method of dividing land into squares and grids.
redemption period a time frame when an owner can buy back real estate that was foreclosed.
redlining illegal action of refusing to lend money to an individual in a lower socio-economic area without considering the circumstances of the individual.
refinance transaction obtaining a new loan on real estate and paying off the first loan using the same real estate as collateral.
Regulation Z federal requirement that a lender must disclose all terms of a loan, including the APR.
release clause a section in a contract that allows the buyer to pay off part of the loan, which then frees a piece of the real estate from the loan.
remainder estate the real estate that passes to another individual when the first individual's rights in the real estate end.
remainderman the individual who real estate goes to when a life tenant dies.
remaining balance the amount still left to pay on a loan.
remaining term the length of time still left to pay on a loan.
rent payment for temporary use of property; lease.
replacement cost the amount of money needed to replicate an edifice so that it can fulfill previous functions.
reproduction cost the amount of money needed for an exact replica of an edifice.
rescission the negating of a contract so that it is no longer in effect.
restriction (restrict covenant) prevents the real estate from being used in certain manners, either in the deed or through local laws.
reversion the landlord's right to take possession of rental property when the rental agreement ends.
reversionary interest the interest the remainderman has in the ownership of the real estate as it passes to them when a life tenant dies.
reverse annuity mortgage a property loan used for a person with high equity when the lender makes yearly payments to the home owner.
revision alteration or change (e.g. contract).
right of egress (or ingress) the right to leave real estate; the right to go to real estate.
right of first refusal the option an individual or entity has to fulfill a legal agreement before another person or entity meets those obligations.
right of redemption the owner's privilege to take possession of real estate when the financial obligations of the loan have been met even during the process of foreclosure.
right of survivorship the remaining survivor's right to take over the interest of the deceased survivor.
riparian rights water rights in close proximity to a person's real estate.

>S

safety clause an extender clause or protection clause that gives the broker commission if a buyer who sees the home returns later to close the sale.

sale-leaseback the sale of the real estate to a new owner and the new owner rents the real estate back to the original owner.
sales contract a legal agreement between a buyer and seller to finalize a sale.
salesperson a professional and licensed real estate agent or broker.
salvage value used to determine depreciation; the worth of a property or asset when its service is over.
satisfaction a document that verifies and confirms the mortgage payoff.
second mortgage a mortgage obtained after the first mortgage used for a down payment, refinancing or cash.
section a unit of measurement in the government rectangular system, one-square mile.
secured loan a loan that uses collateral in the case of default.
security the real estate used as collateral in case of default when money is borrowed.
seisin the owner who holds the title to the property free and clear.
selling broker the real estate agent who finds a buyer for the property.
separate property property that belongs to only one spouse as opposed to both spouses.
servient tenement property that gives shared use of land to a neighboring property for their good.
setback a boundary away from the edge of the property that must remain free of buildings.
settlement statement (HUD-1) a full accounting of all the monetary transactions that occur in a property sale.
severalty independent interest of real estate by a person.
special assessment a financial levy against real estate to pay for something of benefit to that real estate.
special warranty deed a deed that pertains only to the title under the person issuing it, not to any title issues from previous title holders.
specific lien a mortgage or lien against only a specified part of the real estate.
specific performance mandate by the court that the party in a contract fulfill their duties.
standard payment calculation a process of calculating monthly equal payments needed to pay the balance owed on a mortgage at the present interest rate.
statute of frauds legal necessity for real estate contracts to be written.
statute of limitations a time period after which someone cannot file a law suit.
statutory lien a legal obligation on the property, such as taxes.
steering illegal action when only certain racial or cultural groups are shown a property.
straight-line depreciation the total depreciation divided by the number of years of depreciation.
subdivision a division of land into lots upon which homes are built.
sublet to rent from another renter.
subordinate a lesser priority, as in a subordinate mortgage that would be paid off only if the first mortgage was satisfied in a foreclosure.
substitution replacing the market worth of one piece of real estate for another piece of real estate, usually viewed as indifferent by buyers.
subrogation the legal substitution of one individual for another individual, with all rights passing onto the new party.
suit for possession eviction lawsuit after a break of contract by a renter.

suit for specific performance a lawsuit filed by the buyer for breach of contract in property sale. The court can either require the seller to pay damages and expenses or complete the sale.
survey the boundaries of a parcel of real estate; a map of the property surveyed.
syndicate a group of people or entities who join resources to invest in real estate.

>T

tax deed a legal document that places a claim on real estate because of owed taxes.
tax lien a hold placed on real estate because of owed taxes prior to filing the tax deed.
tax rate the rate at which an individual property is taxed; calculated by dividing all funds needed by all properties within the locale.
tax sale the sale of real estate because taxes have not been paid.
tenancy at sufferance a renter who can no longer legally remain on the property because the lease has ended.
tenancy at will an agreement the owner provides to the renter that ends upon if and when the landlord decides to end it. The renter can also terminate the lease.
tenancy by the entirety equal rights to property shared between spouses, the real estate passes to the surviving spouse upon death of a spouse.
tenancy in common equal rights to property shared between individuals without surviving rights but determined through a will upon one party's death.
tenant renter who pays the landlord a fee for property use.
tenement a fixture that remains as part of the land.
testate a person who dies with a legal will in place.
"Time is of the essence" following a contract according to time specifications to prevent delays in fulfilling the contract.
time sharing a piece of real estate owned by more than one person; each person has the right to a specific time at the property.
title legal proof and verification of property ownership.
title insurance insurance that covers the owner from problems with the title.
title search scrutiny of legal records to review the rights to and encumbrances against real estate.
Torrens system a short-cut type of title registration available in some jurisdictions without going through the lengthy process of a title search.
township a section of land in the government rectangular survey system; six-square miles.
trade fixtures fixtures, such as furniture and appliances, used in a specific business; may convey with the property upon the expiration of the lease.
transfer tax an assessment levied when a title passes from one person or entity to another.
trust a holding that transfers the real estate to the trustee for the beneficiary.
trustee the person who keeps the real estate for the beneficiary.
Truth-in-Lending Law federal requirement that a lender must disclose all terms of a loan, including the APR.

>U

underwriting similar to insuring; validating the policy.
undivided interest shared rights and ownership of property among all owners.
unilateral contract one party has a duty to fulfill a certain responsibility in the contract but the other party does not.
unsecured loan a loan that uses no collateral but may be based on the borrower's credit worthiness.
useful life the period of time during which improvements will yield income.
usury charging a higher than maximum interest rate; illegal.

>V

VA-guaranteed loan a mortgage backed by the government agency, the Veteran's Administration, which promises repayment to the lender for the main residence.
valid contract a legally binding contract that will hold up in a court of law.
valuation estimation of the price of real estate.
variance a deviation from zoning laws that permits the owner to violate zoning code.
vendee buyer of personal property.
vendor seller of personal property.
village a small grouping of residential properties and other buildings.
void contract a written agreement that cannot be enforced even when signed.
voidable contract a written agreement that becomes unenforceable after it is signed.

>W

waiver the abdication of certain rights.
warranty deed a legal right of protection against any type of claim.
waste specified abuse of mortgage or rental property that causes damages.
will legal document that transfers ownership of property to another upon the death of the person who writes the will.
wraparound mortgage a property loan that combines a first mortgage with a second mortgage at a higher loan amount and higher payment.
writ of execution an order that permits the court to sell the person's real estate, such as after a foreclosure.

>Z

zone a section regulated by local rules and conditions, such as a business zone that is prohibited from residential housing.
zoning ordinance a regulation that specifies the type of property use permitted in the area.

Real Estate Sales Exam I

1. A couple executes a sales contract on their home after several counter-offers with the buyer. In this case, the seller is:

a) the mortgagee

b) the grantor

c) the grantee

d) the mortgagor

2. The Cambridge family bought a house with a lot size of .25 of an acre. This is equivalent to:

a) 10,890 feet

b) 43,560 feet

c) 11,000 feet

d) 5,250 feet

3. A primary residence is sold for $527,000 by a couple in the 28% tax bracket. The home was originally purchased 8 years ago for $313,000 where the family lived there the entire 8 years. How much will be paid in capital gains?

a) $59,920

b) $32,100

c) $ 214,000

d) none of the above

4. An owner-occupied 4 unit dwelling worth $525,000 generates $4500 in income from 3 units and $150/mo from the onsite laundry. If the current owner typically yields roughly 9% annually on his investment, what is the monthly effective gross amount?

a) $4350

b) $6000

c) $4905

d) $4650

5. A brother is moving out of the country and decides to sell his home to his sister for $275,000, making this the latest sale in that area. The sister decides to pay cash, as she says she will later get a home equity loan for $200,000. Recent sales comps of very similar homes had values of $325,000. Based on the information provided, what is best estimate of the market value of the subject property?

a) $325,000

b) $200,000

c) $275,000

d) not enough information provided

6. When can a landlord choose to **not** rent to someone with children?

a) Never, children are protected under Fair Housing

b) If the unit has evidence of lead paint

c) A lease of an owner occupied 3- family home

d) Someone on a temporary lease

7. A seller provides written permission allowing his listing broker (who has a fiduciary obligation to the seller) to work with the buyer. This relationship is known as:

a) Dual agency

b) Sub agency

c) Special agency

d) Implied agency

8. A homeowner purchased a home for $300,000 on a 30 year FHA loan with an interest rate of 4.25%. If he wants to do cash out conventional refinance and eliminate the MIP, what is the max amount that the new loan balance can be based on a future home value of $350,000?

a) $276,500

b) $310,000

c) $300,000

d) $240,000

9. A valid contract is _____.

a: Verbal agreement
b: A 10 month lease

a) both a and b

b) b only

c) neither a nor b

d) a only

10. A brother is moving out of the country and decides to sell his home to his sister for $275,000, making this home the latest sale in that area. This sister puts 20% down and

finances $220,000. Recent sales comps of similar homes had values of $485,000. Based on the information provided, what is the market value?

a) $485,000

b) $220,000

c) $225,000

d) not enough information provided

11. Which best describes an example of emblements?

a) cherry tree, apple tree and tomato plants

b) cherry tree, apple tree and peach tree

c) tomato, lettuce and onion crops

d) none of these

12. Nine states recognize this system of property ownership where the husband and wife have equal interest in property acquired through marriage. This is _____.

a) common-law

b) community property

c) commingling

d) common title

13. A dad who owns his house free and clear decides to take out a HELOC and let his son make the payments. He also signs a quitclaim deed to transfer the home into his son's name. What clause might the lender enforce?

a) co-insurance clause

b) acceleration clause

c) due-on-sale clause

d) cancellation clause

14. A couple in Indiana requests the name of an excellent home inspector from their agent. All are things the realtor should do EXCEPT which of the following?

a) provide them with a brochure

b) tell them that it is a conflict for her to recommend an inspector

c) give them a list of at least 5 home inspectors

d) direct them to the state home inspection website

15. The Federal Home Loan Mortgage Corporation primarily purchases which loan types:

a) FHA

b) owner-financed notes

c) VA

d) conventional

16. Sally works for ABC Bank. Her job duties are to gather documents, review application for accuracy, package the loan and take each file from pre-approval to closing. What is most likely her job title?

a) underwriter

b) processor

c) loan officer

d) appraiser

17. Which of the following does not loan money directly to borrowers?

a) insurance company

b) mortgage broker

c) cooperative bank

d) private lender

18. Jay decides that he's ready to move out of his parent's home and purchase his own home. He has a roommate who will be moving in so he would like at least a 3 bedroom house. What should his 1st step be?

a) get prequalified by submitting a mortgage application

b) purchase new furniture

c) pick out a house

d) purchase a new car to go with the new house

19. Mike and Kathy have $30,000 or 10% down to purchase their 1st home. Their loan officer prequalifies them for several different loan types. They decide to go with the following scenario: purchase price: $300,000 with a loan amount of $300,000 and $6450 funding fee. What type of loan did they choose?

a) conventional

b) FHA

c) VA

d) negative amortization

20. A lender offers you a very low interest of 2.75% in exchange for part of your equity. What type of mortgage is this?

a) balloon

b) shared equity

c) wraparound mortgage

d) equity loan

21. Sellers Keith and Rita execute a standard purchase and sale agreement on November 1st. The contract also states that by Nov 15th their agent should receive a mortgage commitment letter. November 14th, the buyer's agent sends over a letter that the buyer has been unable to secure financing. They should expect:

a) their earnest money deposit back

b) to withdraw from the transaction

c) both a and b

d) a only

22. House and Home Realty Brokerage leased a 2 family residence for $1500/mo for each unit. Tenant 1 wrote a check to cover the 1st month's rent and deposit and tenant 2 paid by money order. Which is the best representation of what the brokerage must do?

a) make and keep a copy of all funds collected from each tenant

b) nothing as long as the broker received the money that is sufficient

c) Only copy the money order because a check is a legal record

d) Tell the tenant to pay the owner directly

23. Kimberly finds the home of her dreams, cozy bungalow built in 1932. Her agent suspects that the home may have lead-based paint. Kimberly has how many days to test for lead-based paint?

a) 5

b) 3

c) 7

d) 10

24. The governor appoints 12 members to the Real Estate Commission. How many members are not licensed agents?

a) 5

b) 0. all are licensed

c) 1

d) 3

25. An appraisal is done on a unique property that sits on 42.5 acres. The approach the appraiser will more than likely use is _____.

a) assumption

b) cost

c) income

d) market data

26. Jill secures a 15 year fixed conventional home loan. This loan was more than likely purchased by which investor?

a) FNMA

b) insurance company

c) an orb

d) GNMA

27. A homeowner has an existing mortgage balance of $120,000 with a mortgage payment of $1375. He puts an ad in the newspaper to sell his home, owner financing where he will offer the buyer a new note based on a sales price of $258,000 at 5 %. The buyer decides to use this financing to purchase the home. Based on the information given, what type of mortgage is this?

a) wraparound mortgage

b) junior mortgage

c) package mortgage

d) none of these

28. When determining whether a buyer is a good credit risk, the lender needs to evaluate:

a) borrower's credit, the borrower's ability to pay, and homeowner's age

b) ability to pay, property, borrower's 401K

c) borrower's credit, future expected value of the property, job stability

d) property, ability to pay, credit

29. When a buyer chooses to pay discount points, her goal is to receive_____.

a) cash back at closing

b) a lower interest rate

c) principal reduction

d) none of these

30. Kevin's sister decides she wants to purchase a home and needs to get prequalified. Kevin's sister's best friend James is a loan officer at the bank and tells him once the loan closes he will give him a referral fee. Which statement is true?

a) As long as James gives Kim the HUD information booklet within 3 days, he can pay a referral fee

b) James is protected under RESPA

c) James must disclose the referral amount on the GFE

d) Fees and kickbacks to individuals who do not provide a loan is prohibited

31. Members of the Board of Registration of Real Estate serve a term of _____ years.

a) 5

b) 2

c) 7

D) 10

32. The purpose of which of the following laws is to prohibit discrimination on the basis of race (only) in the sale of real property?

a) MGL 151 B

b) Indiana Consumer Protection Law

c) Federal Civil Rights Act of 1866

d) Federal Fair Housing Act of 1868

33. Another name for a HUD-1 is _____,

a) Good Faith Estimate

b) Uniform Settlement statement

c) Truth-in-Lending document

d) Housing Uniform document

34. A homeowner attempts a refinance on his home only to find out that the home has 2 liens from the previous owner that were never paid off. Who should he contact?

a) The title insurance company

b) the escrow office

c) the loan officer

d) a real estate attorney

35. All listing types below allow the seller the right to sell their property on their own without paying a commission, EXCEPT_____.

a) an exclusive agency

b) Open

c) exclusive right to sell

d) none of the above

36. Kurt receives a letter that an expressway is being built where his property sits. The state offers to purchase his home. What right are they (the state) exerting?

a) escheatment

b) foreclosure

c) adverse possession

d) eminent domain

37. A family leases a home with a pool. The contract states that the owner will pay property taxes and insurance, but the tenant must pay the pool and yard expenses. This is known as a _____ lease.

a) percentage

b) gross

c) net

d) month to month

38. Mr. Green has purchased new energy efficient windows, put weather stripping around the doors and replaced his old wall heater with a new central air and heat system. Mr. Green has _____ his home.

a) weatherized

b) energized

c) overhauled

d) redlined

39. Tenant James is renting a 1 bedroom apartment and his rent will be $923 per month. If the cost to replace the lock and key is $150 and the security deposit is the same as the rent, what is the maximum amount of funds James may be asked to give to the owner?

a) $923

b) $2919

c) $1073

d) $ 1996

40. The total commission for the sale of a $449,000 property is 6%. The listing states that they will offer 3.5% to a co-broker who brings a buyer which ends in a successfully closed transaction. How much will the listing broker net after his sales agent, who is on a 45/55 (listing broker gets 55%) split, is paid?

a) $26,940

b) $15,715

c) $6174

d) $11,225

41. Several first time home buyers purchasing homes in a community redevelopment area noticed that they were not offered a fixed rate loan by the developer's lender. They were only offered adjustable rate mortgages. This is most likely an example of _____.

a) economic adjustments

b) redlining

c) conforming

d) steering

42. Susie has been a licensed sales agent for over a year and would like to pursue her broker's license. What must she do?

a) pass the test

b) be a resident of Indiana

c) be at least 18 years old

d) all of the above

43. All are true except:

a) real estate licenses are valid for 4 years

b) an inactive sales agent cannot collect referral fees

c) the fee for renewing a salesperson's license is $40.50

d) a salesperson must take continuing education in order to remain in active status

44. FHA insured loans protect the:

a) lender

b) realtor

c) seller

d) buyer

45. GCA relates to which residence type?

a) 3-family home

b) SFR

c) condo

d) mixed use property

46. A tenant signs a 1 year lease where the owner allows him to occupy the property during this time. This is an example of _____.

a) fee simple

b) freehold estate

c) time share

d) non-freehold estate

47. What is the form used in Indiana when the landlord wants the tenant to either comply with the terms of the lease or leave the premises?

a) Notice to vacate

b) Notice to Quit

c) Notice of Compliance

d) Notice of Eviction

48. When someone who is upside down with their mortgage gets permission to sell their house for less than they owe, this process is known as:

a) short sale

b) foreclosure

c) deed restructure

d) deed-in-lieu of foreclosure

49. "OLD CAR" stands for:

a) obligation, litigation, disclosure, care, access, real estate

b) obedience, loyalty, dedication, confidentiality, accountability, realtor

c) obligation, license, disclosure, confidentiality, accountability, reasonable care

d) obedience, loyalty, disclosure, confidentiality, accountability, reasonable care

50. A couple's agent takes them to see a for-sale by owner listing. The couple decides they really like the house and make an offer. The seller, impressed by the agent's professionalism, asks if she can represent him also. This type of agency is known as _____.

a) facilitator

b) is prohibited in Indiana

c) dual agency

d) buyers agent

51. A broker's license can be revoked if he:

a) fails to return deposit funds to client when requested

b) commingles business and personal funds

c) fails to pay the agent his commission split

d) all of the above

52. A person dies leaving no will and no heirs. The decedent's property would transfer by:

a) adverse possession

b) state

c) escheat

d) laws of descent

53. Describe the ownership of a property if 4 cousins, Keenan, Kelly, Shon, and Marcia are joint tenants and Marcia sells her interest to cousin Michael. The new deed will read:

a) tenants in common with Keenan, Kelly and Shon

b) tenants in will

c) joints tenant Keenan, Kelly and Shon

d) Marcia is not allowed to sell her interest

54. A transaction where the seller agrees to finance the loan of the buyer is called:

a) hard money loan

b) blanket mortgage

c) conventional loan

d) purchase money mortgage

55. A 2,980 square feet home sells for $328,000. If it sits on an acre lot, what is the price/ square feet the home sold for?

a) $94

b) $110

c) $116

d) $154

56. A lot recently sold for $198,000. It is 378' x 296'. What was the cost/acre?

a) $67,074

b) $70,774

c) $77,774

d) $77,042

57. If Michelle sells her home, but then remains in the property by becoming a tenant of the new landlord, this is known as

a) testate

b) wraparound mortgage

c) leaseback

d) freehold

58. A homeowner puts a $104,250 down payment on a $417,000 home. What percentage is the down payment?

a) 25%

b) 18%

c) 20%

d) 30%

59. Matthew sells his home to Sam. Who pays for the transfer tax?

a) Matthew

b) Sam

c) a and b

d) neither

60. An investor gets a 30 year loan due in 15 years. This is a:

a) VA loan

b) package mortgage

c) balloon

d) open-end mortgage

61. In order for Farah, an Indiana real estate broker, to renew her license she must

a) complete 24 hrs of continuing education

b) complete 16 hrs of continuing education

c) complete 20 hrs of his continuing education

d) retake the real estate exam

62. The most probable price that an informed purchaser might pay is the:

a) sales price

b) broker price opinion

c) market value

d) assessed value

63. A lender prequalifies a couple for a loan amount up to $375,000 with a 3.5% down payment. What booklet must he give them within 3 days of application?

a) an information booklet prepared by HUD

b) a booklet on the explanation of closing costs

c) Regulation – Z booklet

c) HUD-1 booklet

64. When a borrower makes a down payment less than 20% and gets an FHA loan, what monthly charge should they expect to be added to their mortgage payment?

a) property taxes

b) funding fee

c) mortgage insurance premium

d) equity loan payment

65. _____ backs rural development loans.

a) a life insurance company

b) FHA

c) Freddie Mac

d) Ginnie Mae

66. The sales comparison approach is also known as the:

a) appraisal process

b) market data

c) replacement cost

d) cost

67. "DUST" is a term associated with:

a) licensing

b) title

c) appraisals

d) conformity

68. In Indiana, if there are more homes on the market than buyers, there is:

a) regression

b) more supply than demand

c) substitution

d) law of decreasing return

69. If a 3 family home is valued at $769,000 and the cap rate is 9%, what is the annual net operating income?

a) $69,210

b) $85,444

c) $100,000

d) $71,000

70. Tim inherits his family's farm which has suffered years of neglect. He decides to take an equity loan on the property, so his realtor orders an appraisal. While doing the appraisal, the appraiser sees obvious physical deterioration and also notices that a bathroom was never added to the home, it still has an outhouse. The lack of an inside bathroom is a _____.

a) functional obsolescence

b) physical deterioration

c) economic obsolescence

d) accrued depreciation

71. Another name for the Federal Fair Housing Act is _____.

a) Fair housing

b) Title VIII of the Civil Rights Act of 1968

c) Federal Civil Rights Act of 1866

d) Consumer Protection Law

72. Indiana allows a non-resident to hold a real estate license if they:

a) move to Indiana

b) sign a notarized letter appointing a family member as their attorney-in-fact

c) purchase a 2 family home and keep the unit as their 2nd residence

d) file a power of attorney appointing the chairmen of the board as their attorney-in-fact

73. All of these are grounds for license suspension or revocation EXCEPT

a) commingling personal and business funds

b) acting as an undisclosed dual agent

c) owing no fiduciary duties to clients while acting as a facilitator

d) practicing real estate with an inactive license

74. All have right of survivorship EXCEPT

a) tenancy in common

b) tenancy by entirety

c) joint tenancy

d) none of the above

75. The best form of ownership is:

a) pur autre vie

b) leasehold

c) fee simple

d) freehold

76. Mary and John owned their home as joint tenants until Mary died. Which statement is true?

a) John now has to sell his home.

b) If there is a loan on the property, the lender will call the loan due.

c) John will become the sole owner

d) John will have to move

77. In Indiana an unlicensed person lists his property for sale stating that he is in fact a licensed agent. What might his fine be?

a) $500

b) $1500

c) $1500

d) $20,000

78. A licensed agent who is associated with a brokerage is a:

a) broker

b) salesperson

c) processor

d) escrow agent

79. Overlooked by many homeowners, which is NOT a cost of owning a home?

a) repairs

b) interest paid on the mortgage loan

c) personal property taxes

d) maintenance

80. Which is MOST likely to influence a person's decision to purchase a home in a certain location?

a) street signage

b) school ratings

c) high number of planned unit developments

d) loan types

81. The only time a broker can add personal funds to the escrow account is

a) never

b) to maintain a minimum balance in the escrow account

c) to purchase investment property using the escrow account

d) if a purchaser asks the broker to hold funds

82. Indiana is a _____ contract state.

a) 1

b) 2

c) 4

d) 3

83. Mr. and Mrs. Sellers signed the purchase and sales agreement in which they are selling their home to the Buyer family. The Buyers have moved forward in getting all inspections, appraisals etc ordered on the property, however the Sellers are now feeling sad and desire to terminate the contract. Which statement is true?

a) they are the owners and maintain the right to terminate the contract at any time

b) they may be forced to sell their home as the contract is legal and binding

c) if they offer to return the buyers deposit and pay other incurred expenses the Buyers must accept this and allow them to terminate the contract

d) none of the above are true

84. Which of the following ads will require more disclosures?

a) We have no money down loans

b) VA, FHA and conventional loans offered here

c) APR is 4.5% on a 30 year fixed loan

d) The interest rate is 4.375% per year

85. A missing _____ could cause a home to not pass an FHA inspection.

a) refrigerator

b) freestanding stove

c) cooktop

d) washer/dryer

86. Larry is purchasing a home that has $20,000 in needed repairs but he doesn't have $20,000. What loan is a good option for him?

a) FHA 203(b)

b) FHA 203(k)

c) FHA 203(c)

d) FHA

87. The minimum age in Indiana to receive a salesperson's license is:

a) 21

b) 25

c) 16

d) 18

88. In Indiana when an agent provides information that another agent has requested, this term is known as:

a) cooperate

b) equity share

c) co-broker

d) commission split

89. In Indiana, a salesperson can work as a(n):

a) employee of the broker

b) independent contractor under the broker

c) a and b

d) neither

90. A Indiana law that protects consumers is:

a) MGL chapter 151 B

b) 21 E certificate

c) Consumer credit laws

d) Uniform Deceptive Trade Practices Act

91. Jim does a lot of home improvement projects, so he built a shed on his neighbor Jerry's land. Jim has used this shed continuously for over 20 years. Jim can pursue a claim of _____ in order to gain title the property.

a) adverse possession

b) eminent domain

c) servient tenement

d) concurrent ownership

92. An ad reads "2 story traditional 1500 square foot home in Atlanta, Indiana for sale. Asking $423,000. Please call Rhonda at 857-455-8234. From a legal perspective, the ad is missing:

a) Rhonda's last name

b) Rhonda disclosing that she is a broker

c) number of bedrooms and bathrooms

d) Rhonda disclosing her brokerage's name and that she is a licensed broker

93. What is a broker's commission fee percent if she sells a building for $673,225 and her fee earned is $16,830.62?

a) 2.5%

b) 6.5%

c) 3.5 %

d) 4.0%

94. Another name for loan fees is:

a) application fee

b) credit report fee

c) discount points

d) broker's fees

95. The Federal Civil Rights Act was passed in

a) 1968

b) 1866

c) 1868

d) 1986

96. The _____ sets the minimum requirements for appraisals.

a) RESPA

b) MLS

c) TILA

d) USPAP

97. A section is:

a) 2 square miles

b) a city block

c) 27,878,400 square feet

d) 43,560 acres

98. After what year did Indiana mandate that all new or rehabbed 4-family homes or larger 1st floor units be handicap accessible?

a) 1968

b) 1991

c) 2002

d) 1986

99. Which is not covered under the fair housing laws?

a) a SFR that is corporate owned

b) elderly housing that meets certain Department of Housing and Urban Development guidelines

c) a 2-4 unit dwelling that is not owner occupied

d) a home owned by an individual who owns more than 3 properties

100. Within a 3 year period, an owner has been found guilty of sending discriminatory letters to his tenants. The owner may have to pay civil penalties up to _____ if this is his 1st offense:

a) $25,000

b) $10,000

c) $50,000

d) $20,000

Real Estate Sales Exam I Answers

1. b. The couple (owner) is conveying title to the real property.

2. a. 1 acre = 43,560   43,560 * .25 = 10,890 feet

3. d. None of the above. The property is a primary residence which has been lived in over 5 years with a profit less than $500,000.

4. d. The effective gross amt is $4500 + $150 (the sum of all income generated.)

5. a. The transaction is "non-arms length" because they are related.

6. c. The children are generally protected under Chapter 151B (Fair Housing) except when an occupant requests a temporary lease

7. b. Subagency requires that the listing broker obtain written permission from the seller and that the fiduciary duties are to the seller.

8. a. To eliminate the mortgage insurance premium, the loan to value must be below 80%.

9. a. A contract is defined as an agreement between 2 or more persons or entities and they can be written or verbal.

10. a. This is an arm's length transaction because the brother and sister are related; therefore the sold price cannot be included with non-arm's length sales comps.

11. c. Emblements are crops that are annually cultivated.

12. b. Each spouse has equal interest in property acquired during marriage.

13. c. Because the borrower has transferred the property, the lender is allowed to demand full payment.

14. c. In Indiana the agent can not recommend an inspector.

15. d. Fannie Mae and Freddie Mac purchase conventional loans.

16. b. Processors prepare the loan package for the underwriter

17. b. Mortgage brokers bring borrowers together with lenders.

18. a. The 1st step to obtaining home loan financing is to submit the application.

19. c. VA loans offer 100% financing and include a funding fee.

20. b. Shared equity is when the lender offers a low interest rate in exchange for a portion of the equity.

21. c. This contract was written with a financing contingency in which the purchase was given a date to secure financing.

22. a. The property manager is required to make and keep a copy of collected funds for 3 years.

23. d. Under the Lead Paint Law, the buyer gets 10 days to test for evidence of lead paint.

24. d. There are 3 members who are not real estate professionals. Their role is to represent the public.

25. b. The cost approach is used when the appraiser has difficulty finding comps.

26. a. FNMA purchases conventional loans.

27. a. The new mortgage will include the remaining balance on the existing first mortgage.

28. d. The lender must do an appraisal, ensure the borrower has means to repay the mortgage and meet the lender's credit score.

29. b. Points charged by a lender are to lower the rate for the buyer.

30. d. RESPA prohibits several types of payments to persons who did not perform a service.

31. a. The term is for 5 years.

32. c. The Civil Rights Act of 1866 prohibits discrimination on the basis of race in the sale, lease, or other transfer of real or personal property.

33. b. A HUD-1 is also known as a Uniform Settlement Statement.

34. a. The title insurance companies protect the holder from defects in the title.

35. c. An exclusive right to sell listing allows the broker to receive a commission no matter who sells the property.

36. d. Eminent domain gives the government the right to take private property for public use.

37. c. In net lease, the tenant pays the maintenance and operating expenses.

38. a. Because he made energy efficient improvements he has weatherized his home.

39. The maximum a Indiana landlord can charge a new tenant is 1st month's rent + 2nd month's rent + security deposit + cost for new keys and lock change 3 x 923+ 150 =2919.

40. c. Subtract the listing broker's commission from the total commission percentage. Then multiply that number to the home sales price. Then multiply that number by the listing broker's split with his agent.   6- 3.5= 2.5% x 449000 = 11225 x 55% = 6174.

41. b. The lender only offered 1 loan type to homebuyers purchasing in the area which is more than likely a low to moderate income area.

42. d. To be a broker in Indiana she has to pass the test, be at least 18 years old, have been a salesperson for over a year, and be a resident of Indiana.

43. a. Real estate licenses are good for 2, not 4, years in Indiana.

44. a. FHA insured loans protect the lender in the event the borrower defaults.

45. c. Condos are created under MGL 183A in which it provides a permit for multi-unit buildings to be divided into separate units that can be owned by an individual fee simple estate.

46. d. Non-freehold estates give the holder of the estate the right to occupy the property until the end of the lease.

47. b. Notice to Quit forms are used for eviction and/or to tell the tenant to comply with the terms of the lease.

48. a. Short sale is when the bank gives the homeowner the permission to sell the home when they owe more than it's worth.

49. d. "OLD CAR" is an acronym used to remember the agent's fiduciary duties to their client.

50. c. In a dual agency, the broker represents both parties in a transaction.

51. d. A broker cannot mix business and personal funds, refuse to pay client their escrow funds when requested and hold out on paying his sales agent.

52. c. When no heirs can be found, the state can lay claim to the property.

53. a. Joint tenants can transfer title but the new owner becomes a tenant in common with the other joint tenants. For joint tenancy to be valid everyone has to go on title at the same time.

54. d. A purchase money mortgage is when the seller holds the financing for the borrower.

55. b. Price/ square feet is found by dividing the price by the square feet. 328000/2980 = 110.

56. d. Multiply the lot dimensions 378 x 296 = 111,888 square feet. Determine how many acres the lot is. An acre is 43,560 square feet; therefore divide 111,888/ 43,560= 2.57 acres. Divide the cost of $198,000 by 2.57 = $77,042.

57. c. New landlord leases property back to the tenant.

58. a. Divide the down payment by the sales price. 104,250/417000 = .25 or 25%.

59. a. The Commonwealth of Indiana charges tax stamps whenever real property changes hands and this expense is paid by the seller at closing.

60. c. In a balloon mortgage the final lump sum is due at the balloon termination date.

61. a. A broker or sales agent must take 16 hours of continuing education classes within 2 years to renew their license.

62. c. Market value is the most probable price that an informed buyer will pay.

63. a. Per RESPA, a lender or mortgage broker must give a borrower a copy of a HUD prepared information booklet within 3 days of application.

64. c. FHA provides mortgage insurance to protect the lender in case default and the borrower pays a monthly fee along with their mortgage payment.

65. d. The Government National Mortgage Association (Ginnie Mae) is a major purchaser of government-backed mortgage loans.

66. b. The Market Data approach is also known as the Comparison approach.

67. c. DUST is an acronym for the elements that establish value and is associated with appraisals.

Demand for the type of property

Utility (desirable use) the property offers

Scarcity of properties available

Transferability of property to a new owner

68. b. There's a larger inventory of homes than there are buyers

69. a. Value x Cap rate = Net Operating Income

   769000 x .09 = 69210

70. a. Functional obsolescence highlights features that are no longer considered desirable.

71. b. The Federal Fair Housing Act broadened the prohibitions against discrimination in housing to include sex, race, color religion, national origin, and handicap familial status in connection with the sale or rental of housing or vacant land.

72. d. Indiana allows non-residents to hold a real estate license if they file a power of attorney appointing the chairmen of the board as their attorney-in-fact for legal issues relating to that individual.

73. c. A facilitator (non-agent) owes no fiduciary duties to clients

74. a. Tenancy in common does not have right of survivorship. Tenancy by entirety is a form of joint tenancy and has along with joint tenancy right of survivorship.

75. c. Fee simple is a type of freehold estate and is the best form of ownership because the owner has the right to occupy or rent the property, sell or transfer ownership, build on and mine for minerals and restrict or allow the use of the property to others.

76. c. Joint tenancy includes the right of survivorship, the surviving co-owners share equally in the deceased owner's interest.

77. a. The Indiana fine for performing real estate without a license is $500.

78. b. A licensed agent who is associated with a brokerage is a salesperson.

79. c. Personal property taxes are taxes on personal property not real property.

80. b. School ratings can influence whether a person purchases in a certain area.

81. b. A broker can mix business and personal funds if the broker needs to add funds to maintain a minimum balance in the escrow account.

82. a. Indiana is a single contract. The Purchase and Sale Agreement outlines the entire transaction.

83. b. Because the contract is legal and binding, if the Sellers don't move forward, they will be in breach of contract and the Buyers can sue for specific performance.

84. a. The ad should disclose the loan amount, down payment and APR and terms of repayment.

85. c. FHA minimum property guidelines state that the home must be delivered in safe, secure and sound condition. A free standing stove could be considered personal property, but a cooktop (because it is attached) is a part of the home.

86. b. FHA 203(k) is FHA's Rehabilitation Loan Insurance Program.

87. d. Indiana minimum age for a real estate license is 18.

88. a. In real estate when an agent provides information that another agent has requested this is to cooperate.

89. c. The agent can work as an independent contractor or an employee.

90. d. The Indiana Uniform Deceptive Trade Practices Act prohibits unfair and deceptive trade practices and real estate agents and brokers are subject to this.

91. a. Adverse possession is a method of acquiring title to another person's property through court action after continuous use for over 20 years.

92. d. The broker must disclose her name and that she is a licensed broker.

93. a. Divide the total commission earned by the sales price. 16830.62/673225 =.025 x 100 = 2.5%.

94. c. Discount points are loan fees that the buyer can pay to get a lower interest rate.

95. b. The Federal Civil Rights Act was passed in 1866 to prohibit discrimination on the basis of race.

96. d. The Uniform Standards of Professional Appraisal Practice (USPAP) sets the minimum requirement for appraisals.

97. c. A section is 640 acres. (640 acres/acre) x 43560 sq ft = 27,878,400 square feet.

98. b. The Federal Fair Housing Act of 1968 prohibits discrimination against mentally or physically handicapped individuals. Then after 1991 it was mandated that all new or rehabbed four-family homes or larger must be designed so the 1st floor units include handicapped accessibility.

99. b. The Federal Fair Housing Act does not cover housing for the elderly that meets certain HUD guidelines.

100. b. Under the Federal Fair Housing Act a person can pay civil penalties up to $10,000 for the 1st offense.

Real Estate Sales Exam II

1. MY TOWN Realty gets a listing to sell a home. The broker appoints one of his sales agents (with permission of the sellers), Melissa represent the sellers. During one of the open houses, a couple comes in and decides to make an offer, so they call the broker at MY TOWN, who then assigns one of his other sales agents, Keith to represent the buyers. In this case the broker is acting as a:

a) non-agent

b) designated seller's and buyer's agent/dual agent

c) single agent

d) principal agent

2. A buyer secures a 1st mortgage for $243,750, puts down 15% and the seller carry's back 10%. What was the sales price of the home if she paid full asking?

a) $250,000

b) $300,000

c) $375,000

d) $325,000

3. All are true statements regarding appraisal reports EXCEPT?

a) they can be verbally delivered

b) they must be delivered on the Uniform Residential Appraisal Report

c) must use guidelines set forth by USPAP

d) they can be delivered in writing

4. Seller competition in the market usually results in:

a) higher home prices

b) lower home prices

c) anticipation

d) progression

5. The disposition, control, right of possession and enjoyment are all:

a) zoning ordinances

b) Intangibles

c) corporeal

d) the bundle of rights of ownership

6. All are real property EXCEPT

a) air rights

b) refrigerator

c) oak tree

d) pond

7. Jack is unable to secure financing to purchase the Indiana home he made an offer on; therefore the contract was not consummated. Which Supreme Court decision implies that that the seller will not have to pay commission in this case?

a) Brown v Board of Education

b) 485 Lafayette Street

c) Tristam's Landing

c) Sherman Anti-trust Law

8. A church, which has 501(c) 3 status is exempt from paying:

a) a mortgage

b) property taxes

c) hazard insurance

d) licensing fees

9. Anthony sells his condo to Michael. Besides getting a certified letter from the condo association, what other certificate must he obtain?

a) insurance

b) 21(e)

c) property tax

d) freehold

10. Matthew decides to purchase a home, so he gives his landlord of 2 years a 30 day notice. If his security deposit was $1345 and the bank interest rate (where the landlord held his deposit) was 1%, how much money should he expect back?

a) 1545.38

b) $1345

c) $1358.45

d) $1435

11. Even though Jennifer's lease ended over a month ago, she has not moved out. What type of tenancy does she now have?

a) tenancy at will

b) tenancy for years

c) tenancy for period to period

d) tenancy at sufferance

12. Realtors are members of the

a) NAREB

b) NRA

c) NAR

d) REBAC

13. A lender needs to set a listing price on one of their foreclosed homes. They will more than likely order a(n):

a) mortgage payment history

b) appraisal

c) assessed value report

d) BPO

14. Which one is an example of commercial real estate?

a) a 21 unit apartment complex

b) a store for rent

c) a store front with apartments on the second floor

d) loft apartments

15. Julian refuses to pay his condo association fees; he runs the risk of the association placing a priority lien on his property. This Bill is known as the

a) Priority Lien

b) 6(d) certificate

c) Indiana General Laws 183A

d) Super Lien

16. Fructus naturales refers to:

a) real property

b) emblements

c) natural fruit

d) annually cultivated crops

17. An exploration company purchases the rights to any minerals and oil from an owner. The owner now owns all rights EXCEPT the following

a) subsurface

b) water

c) air

d) surface

18. In Indiana a manufactured home is proven by:

a) mortgage deed

b) mortgage note

c) bill of sale

d) purchase contract

19. Cheri was so happy when she received checks from her lender where she could use them to pay her contractor. She took out a(n) _____ mortgage.

a) equity

b) land sales

c) purchase money mortgage

d) primary

20. Bill negotiated the lease for his new apartment on the phone and told the landlord that he could sign the lease and meet in person within 3 days. However, Bill experienced an emergency and had to fly out of town right away, so he told his twin brother Will to meet the landlord and sign the lease for him. The lease is:

a) valid

b) void

c) voidable

d) illegal

21. In 2 days, Jackie was anticipating going to her home loan closing, but instead she received a call from her agent that the home had an old 2nd lien on it that the seller said he paid off. What term best describes the title?

a) the title is free and clear

b) the title is encumbered

c) the title is vested

d) the title is clouded

22. Due to the economy and a loss of jobs in the area. Home prices have fallen by 46% and are now valued at about $372,000. Based on the information, what was the average home price?

a) $866,000

b) $689,000

c) $668,000

d) $888,888

23. Janet's landlord locked her out of the building she lives in Marietta, Indiana. She decides that she wants to file a lawsuit against him but finds that he has filed bankruptcy. She must file her case with which court?

a) Janet cannot file a lawsuit; she must go before the bankruptcy court

b) Judicial

c) Housing

d) District

24. A couple, who had their home listed with Any Town Brokerage, hosted a Christmas party. One of the guests from the party loved the home and came back over to ask them several questions about the house and get a formal tour. He ended up purchasing the home and the sellers did not have to pay Any Town Brokerage any commission. What type of listing did they have with Any Town?

a) dual

b) net

c) open

d) exclusive agency

25. An apartment purchaser receives shares and a limited partnership. What type of apartment was purchased?

a) condo

b) cooperative

c) multi unit

d) 3 family home

26. 17 year old Arthur, a college student, is told by a landlord that he is too young to rent one of his apartments. Which Indiana state law might the landlord be violating?

a) GL 21(e)

b) Equal Housing Act

c) Fair Housing Act

d) Uniform Deceptive Trade Practices Act

27. Balance contributes to value when:

a) there is homogeneity in a neighborhood

b) there are diverse land uses

c) there is conformity

d) there is regression

28. If an agent is found to have violated Indiana fair housing laws, he may be required to pay damages up to _____ times those incurred by the victim.

a) 3

b) 120

c) 30

d) 9

29. Mrs. Tenant vacated her apartment because her landlord turned off the water. This was a(n):

a) adverse eviction

b) lease back

c) constructive eviction

d) contractual eviction

30. In a 99-year lease, the buyer typically receives all bundle of rights EXCEPT:

a) enjoyment

b) possession

c) control of use

d) none of the above

31. Missy paid her landlord the 1st month's rent and a security deposit. What does Indiana state law mandate that he give her?

a) thank you letter

b) keys immediately

c) list of tenant rules

d) receipt

32. How long must receipts for rental payments, including canceled checks or money orders, be kept by a broker in Indiana?

a) 30 days past the end of the lease.

b) 3 years.

c) 1 year

d) 10 years past the termination of the lease

33. In Indiana, what type of tenancy does a tenant who lives in public housing have if they have additional tenant protections?

a) tenant at will

b) tenant with written lease

c) tenant by regulation

d) tenant at sufferance

34. Another name for a tenant at will is _____.

a) yearly lease

b) common tenancy

c) sublease

d) month to month

35. In a Indiana mobile home park transaction, if the landlord acts as the seller's sales agent, the landlord's fee cannot exceed _____%.

a) 6

b) 3.5

c) 5

d) 10

36. The _____ requires that all Purchase and Sale Agreements must be in writing.

a) National Association of Realtors

b) Indiana Statue of Frauds

c) US Dept of Housing and Urban Development

d) Indiana License Law

37. A seller will pay 3% in closing cost. If the sales price is $378,499 and the buyer is putting down a 20% down payment, which is the amount paid by the seller?

a) $ 2270

b) $9084

c) $3000

d) $11,355

38. Indiana property managers must have a:

a) broker's license

b) 2-year degree

c) real estate salesperson's license

d) none of the above

39. Mike and Dana are renting a unit in their 1946 2 family home to a couple with a 5 year old child. What must they (Mike and Dana) do in accordance to the Lead Law?

a) delead

b) give the new tenants a Lead Paint Notice

c) have the tenants sign an escalation lease

d) provide the tenants a stock certificate

40. Stan and his business partner decide to sell their 4 unit property. They find another 4 unit property in a town closer to where they live which will make it easier to manage. What product can they use that may ease their current tax burden from the sale?

a) 1031 exchange

b) owner financing

c) hard money loan

d) equity loan

41. If you are a tenant in a property that has been foreclosed, your tenancy will:

a) terminate and you must immediately move out

b) automatically convert to a written lease with the lender

c) automatically turn into a tenancy at will

d) turn into an option to purchase

42. Sharon was told that her front and back end numbers were 48/55 and that she did not qualify for a home loan at this time. These are called _____.

a) LTV

b) qualifying ratios

c) cost per unit

d) income to debt ratios

43. Farmer Jedd has _____ rights in that he is able to allow his horses to drink from the river next to his property.

a) mineral

b) air and surface

c) littoral

d) riparian

44. In Indiana, when 2 people are co-owners on a property, the 3 types of ownership are:

a) tenancy in common, tenancy in sufferance and tenancy as written

b) joint tenancy, tenancy at will and tenancy in common

c) tenancy by the entirety, tenancy in common, and joint tenancy

d) tenancy in common, tenancy by the entirety and tenancy in sufferance

45. An agent lost her wallet with her real estate license. In order to get a duplicate, she must_____.

a) complete the change of name form on the Board's website

b) misplaced license form

c) retake the test

d) only send in the applicable fee, no form is needed.

46. Mitzi is a licensed agent but no longer wishes to perform real estate. The **only** thing she needs to do is:

a) send a resignation letter to her broker

b) send a resignation letter to the Board

c) do not pay the renewal fee

d) tell the Board members in person when they have a meeting

47. In Indiana, a 1st time homebuyer is someone who hasn't owned a property for _____ years.

a) 4

b) 5

c) never owned a home

d) 3

48. The Taxpayer Relief Act was passed in:

a) 1997

b) 1986

c) 1977

d) 2001

49. Flood insurance is

a) always optional

b) required in certain areas

c) automatically included in the hazard insurance policy

d) only available to homeowners purchasing properties financed by rural housing

50. Patty has gotten a loan pre- approval from **Conservative** Trust Bank. More than likely, her housing expense ratio does not exceed _____ percent.

a) 38

b) 20

c) 28

d) 33

51. For keeping real estate contracts in Indiana, _____ years is the Contract Law Statute of Limitations.

a) 1

b) 3

c) 6

d) 8

52. Under the cost approach, the formula for determining value is:

a) Replacement or reproduction cost – Accrued Depreciation + Land Value = Value

b) Accrued Depreciation – Replacement or reproduction cost + Land Value = Value

c) Replacement or reproduction cost + Accrued Depreciation - Land Value = Value

d) Replacement or reproduction cost + Land Value – Accrued Depreciation = Value

53. All are examples of a protected class EXCEPT:

a) children

b) veterans

c) elderly

d) All of the above

54. A broker told an elderly couple that for $3000 she could help them get their loan modified to a more affordable payment, but after the couple gave her the money she disappeared. What Indiana law has the broker violated?

a) The Federal Civil Rights Act

b) The Indiana General Law Chapter 151B

c) Indiana Lead Paint Law

d) Indiana Consumer Protection Law (Chapter 93A)

55. The _____ pledges the property as collateral.

a) mortgage lien

b) mortgage deed

c) mortgage note

d) collateralization note

56. Land, "bundle of legal rights", and permanent, human-made additions are

a) personal property

b) emblements

c) real property

d) real estate

57. Lisa and Mike are remodeling their home. The contractor unloads a truckload of drywall and tile in front of their house. The delivered items are

a) personal property

b) encumbrances

c) real property

d) real estate

58. Which is **Not** one of the "bundle of rights"?

a) right to transfer the home to a relative

b) right to live in the home

c) right to refuse entry into the home

d) right to run a neighborhood casino

59. Which economic characteristic of Real Estate best represents the following example? Two identical homes built by the same developer are located on Milford Street, which is a street that separates 2 cities, Old City and New City. House A is in New City and sits on the west side of the street and house B sits on the east side of the street and is in Old City. Because it is a newer area, homeowner's believe that the school district in New City is better than Old City.

a) relative scarcity

b) area preference

c) supply and demand

d) improvements

60. A granddaughter inherited a home worth about $225,000 that her grandparents lived in for 50 years. This home had a great deal of sentimental value to her so because of this she decided to remodel the home to her taste, which costs her well over $380,000 in remodeling costs. While the home's value did increase to $300,000, the appraiser did tell her that she over-improved the home for that neighborhood. What type of value does this home now have?

a) objective

b) indestructible

c) subjective

d) immobility

61. In Indiana a brokerage can exist under a temporary broker's license without examination when:

a) the broker travels out of the country

b) the broker decides to appoint one of his agents as a broker

c) the broker is late in completing his continuing education and paying the renewal fee

d) the broker of record passes away

62. A Indiana broker acting on behalf of a developer of an out of state real estate development has to notify the Commission in writing of their status within _____ days of accepting the client.

a) 7

b) 2

c) 5

d) 10

63. Who can issue a junior mortgage?

a) Freddie Mac

b) the VA

c) the seller

d) RHS

64. Kelley, Marvin and Andrea are joint tenants. When Andrea dies, Kelley and Marvin remain as joint tenants. When Marvin dies, Kelley now holds title as a sole owner. Kelley now holds title in _____.

a) common

b) severalty

c) entirety

d) life estate

65. Greg has an ocean front property where he is able to freely enjoy the ocean at any time. He has _____ rights.

a) bundle of rights

b) alluvion

c) riparian

d) littoral

66. A _____ is divided into 36 sections.

a) city

b) township

c) Commonwealth

d) acre

67. In a deed, **ET ux** means

a) and wife

b) everyone

c) and others

d) and husband

68. Abraham bought a property and later learned that his great grandfather's father may have owned that property. What can he order that will show the property ownership history?

a) deed of trust

b) legal description

c) certificate of title

d) chain of title

69. A chattel mortgage would more than likely be used in a transaction with all of the following EXCEPT

a) car

b) furniture

c) single family residence

d) mobile home

70. A developer plans to build a new subdivision that is pedestrian friendly. The homes will be on small lots, but the community will have several "green" areas with parks and common areas for the residents. This type of design is known as _____.

a) communal property

b) clustering

c) commingling

d) canvassing

71. Mrs. James' husband passed away about 6 months ago and because she is on fixed income she is finding it difficult to meet all of her expenses due to her husband's remaining medical bills. Because she owns her home free and clear and she would like to remain in it, what loan product might be a good option for her?

a) junior mortgage

b) HELOC

c) primary mortgage

d) HECM

72. Which is NOT a method used to satisfy the requirement for legal description in a deed.

a) the Torrens System

b) the metes and bounds system

c) the lot and block system

d) the government survey system

73. Juliet has lived in her apartment for 4 months and loves it. Because summer is approaching and she does not have air conditioning, she's decided to replace her dining room lighting fixture with a ceiling fan. The ceiling fan will now be a(n)

a) riparian right

b) easement

c) real property

d) personal property

74. A hardship associated with acquiring rental property is

a) the law of increasing returns

b) lack of reserves

c) negative amortization

d) redlining

75. A broker's license is NOT required

a) when an individual sells his candy store business to another individual

b) when he offers to list real property for sale

c) when he offers to sell his parents' home

d) in exchange for 1 month's rent, negotiate the rental of real estate for another individual

76. The ADA is the

a) American Disabled Vets Act

b) American Disposition of Realty Act

c) American Disposal Act

d) American with Disabilities Act

77. Misty works as a sales agent under Real Time Realty in which she is an independent contractor. She should expect all of the following EXCEPT:

a) to assume responsibility for paying her own income tax

b) to compensated on production

c) to receive employee benefits from the broker

d) that she and the broker will have a written contract

78. Manny and Lisa purchased their home 6 years ago for $325,000 where they put down 10%. Their interest rate was 6.5% and after making 72 monthly payments, their loan balance was $268,901.06. Assuming the current market value and the sales price are the same, how much equity does the homeowner have?

a) $32,500

b) $56,098.04

c) $29,200

d) none of the above

79. Every homeowner is entitled to the following income tax deductions EXCEPT

a) loan interest on second homes

b) property taxes

c) discount points

d) penalty-fee withdrawals up to $10,000 from an IRA

80. Byron, a first time homebuyer, bought his home for $72,500 with an FHA loan. The contract was executed April 28th, 2010. Because he had a 60 day escrow, he finally got his keys on June 30th, 2010. How much tax credit money should he expect to get back if he has no other tax liabilities?

a) $7,250

b) $500

c) $8000

d) $7500

81. Which physical characteristic of real estate best describes the following: 2 parcels of land are not identical

a) homogeneity

b) immobility

c) nonhomogeneity

d) a physical characteristic of land

82. All are uses of real property EXCEPT

a) residential

b) grazing cattle

c) cemetery

d) all of the above

83. The first real estate license law was passed in _____ in 1919.

a) Indiana

b) New York

c) California

d) Texas

84. A cookie shop owner needs to move to a larger location. When he removed the oven, he repaired the holes from the bolts on the walls and the floors. The oven was a(n)

a) fixture

b) trade fixture

c) real property

d) appurtenance

85. The section on the 1003 that deals with the race or ethnicity and sex of an application is data collected under the

a) Home Mortgage Disclosure Act

b) Community Redevelopment Act

c) Fair Housing Act

c) Federal Civil Rights Act

86. Broker Connie says the following phrases to her clients, "Better sell the house before too many of them move in the neighborhood", "There goes the neighborhood". These are examples of

a) redlining

b) steering

c) blockbusting

d) commingling

87. Randy meets with loan officer Jackie so she can prequalify him for a loan. After talking with Randy she learns that he is unmarried and decides to halt the application process. Randy calls her several times only to receive a voicemail. Since it appears as though Jackie is discriminating against Randy on the basis of marital status, what law is she violating?

a) The Civil Rights Act of 1964

b) The ADA

c) The Federal Fair Housing Act of 1866

d) ECOA

88. Which is NOT a purpose of the License Law?

a) raise revenue

b) to protect the public from incompetent brokers

c) prescribe minimum standards for licensing brokers

d) protect licensed brokers and salespersons from unfair or improper competition

89. Which is the best acronym to help in remembering the 4 government powers?

a) DUST

b) OldCAR

c) PETE

d) PPEDTE

90. Ms. Mary owned the land adjacent to her church and decided to grant it to the church so long as it is used to build a recreation center for the church's youth. This type of estate is known as

a) fee simple

b) determinable fee

c) legal fee

d) conventional life estate

91. Sonja gave her $3500 earnest money deposit to her sales agent. What should her sales agent do next?

a) deposit the check in his (sales agents) personal checking account

b) give the check to the office's transaction coordinator who will then put the check in the company's escrow account

c) cash the check and give Sonja a receipt

d) give the check to the office's transaction coordinator who will then place the check in file folder with Sonja's name on it along with the contract and store them safely in the file cabinet

92. Johnny and Donna visit a new home development and fall in love with the model homes. All of the homes in this subdivision will only have 1 level. After picking a floor plan they like, they ask the sales agent what the cost would be to add a 2nd story media room and bathroom. The sales agent advises the couple that the developers have created a _____ _____ that does not permit 2nd story homes in the subdivision.

a) planning and zoning law

b) inverse condemnation

c) public control

d) deed restriction

93. Ted received a letter stating that the lender had obtained a deficiency judgment against him. Which scenario below best fits what has happened to Ted?

a) One of his creditors from a credit card put his account in collections then filed a judgment against him.

b) The home was sold in an auction for the amount he owed, but because there were no funds to pay the agents the lenders paid it and are now suing Ted for the deficiency.

c) Ted's loan balance and fees were more than the home sold for at foreclosure sale; therefore the lender will claim Ted's other assets in order to satisfy the indebtedness.

d) none of the above

94. When working on behalf of a seller or buyer, an agent must exhibit good business judgment, trust and honesty. This creates a(n) _____ _____.

a) fiduciary relationship

b) faithful performance

c) implied authority

d) special agent

95. Keith is selling his 5 unit complex. He should be prepared to bring all documents below EXCEPT:

a) tax returns

b) lease agreements

c) maintenance contracts

d) estoppels letters from the tenants

96. Baker and Johnson Partnership decides to sell off some their real estate. If each partner holds title as tenants in common, which signatures will be required to convey the real estate?

a) Only 1 signature is required since it is a Partnership.

b) Since each partner holds title, they will each have to sign.

c) They can sign with a stamp in the name of their Partnership.

d) Whenever a Partnership sells real estate, only 2 signatures are required no matter how many partners there are.

97. Theron and Perry are neighbors. Theron builds a fence in which 2 feet of it extends into Perry's property. The fence is an example of a(n)

a) eminent domain

b) encumbrance

c) encroachment

d) easement by necessity

98. A couple residing in a community property state have been married for 5 years. During the marriage, the wife's grandfather decides to give each grandchild their inheritance, which is one of his income producing properties. The property is

a) community property

b) sole proprietorship

c) part of a land trust

d) separate property

99. Real estate ownership by a corporation is a(n)

a) tenancy in sufferance

b) tenancy in severalty

c) joint tenancy

d) none of the above as corporations can own real estate

100. Barbara has been pre-approved for a maximum purchase price of $318,000 based on 90% LTV. What will her down payment?

a) $10,000

b) $6400

c) $ 32,000

d) $23,000

Real Estate Sales Exam II Answers

1. b. Designated buyer's and seller's agent is a designated agent who represents their client and owes fiduciary duties to their client and with the client's permission the agent can be designated by another agent. When the appointing agent designates, another agent in the office to represent the other party to the transaction, the broker will also be a dual agent.

2. d. First, we need to establish that the borrower's down payment and the seller carry back can be added together and treated like it is the borrower's down payment. Second, find the loan to value(LTV) which is 100-25=75% or .75 since we are given the loan amount and now have the LTV we can solve for the sales price: $243,750/.75 = $325,000.

3. b. The appraisal can be verbal or written.

4. b. When sellers are competing there is a lot of demand in the market which drives home prices down.

5. d. The bundle of rights are the property rights which include the right of possession, control, enjoyment and disposition.

6. b. The refrigerator is not attached to the house. The owner can take this with him/her therefore it is personal property.

7. c. Tristam's Landing states that a real estate broker under a brokerage agreement is entitled to commission if three requirements are met:

- The broker produces a purchaser ready, to buy on the owner's terms

- The purchaser enters into a binding contract with the owner to purchase the property

- The purchaser completes the transaction by closing the title in accordance with the provisions of the contract

8. b. Non-profits are exempt from paying property taxes.

9. b. Anthony must provide an insurance certificate showing the new owner and his mortgage holder will be covered under the condominium master insurance policy in order to transfer the property, in Indiana.

10. c. In Indiana, the landlord is to give the tenant the interest he earned in the bank on the deposit.

11. a. Tenancy at will is a lease without a termination date

12. c. National Association of Realtors

13. d. BPO or broker price opinion is when the mortgage holder gets a broker's opinion of value based on a competitive market analysis.

14. b. Commercial property is used to produce income.

15. d. The Super Lien Bill gives the association the right to impose a priority lien.

16. a. Fructus naturals are considered to be citrus fruit, apples, berries and grapes and remain with the property.

17. a. Subsurface rights are rights below the earth's surface.

18. c. Manufactured homes are considered personal property as most are not permanently affixed.

19. a. Equity mortgage is where the homeowner takes out a portion of the equity on their property and often times lenders will send the borrower checks.

20. c. A voidable contract binds one party but not the other.

21. d. Clouded title is any document, claim, unreleased lien that may impair the title to real property or make the title doubtful.

22. b. First we need to find the LTV which is 100-46 =54% or .54. $372,000/.54 =$688,889.

23. a. In Indiana if the landlord has filed bankruptcy, the tenant must go before the bankruptcy court.

24. d. An exclusive agency listing means that only 1 listing broker represents the seller. If the property sells through the efforts of the broker, however the seller retains the right to sell the property on their own without paying a commission.

25. b. Cooperatives are apartments owned by a corporation that holds titles to the entire cooperative property.

26. c. The Indiana Fair Housing Act prohibits discrimination on several Protected classes in 2 different Categories. Age is in Category One.

27. b. Balance is when a neighborhood or town has several different types of land uses.

28. a. An agent's may be required to pay up to triple damages if he or she is found to have violated Indiana fair housing laws.

29. c. Constructive eviction is when a landlord has rendered a property uninhabitable and the tenant moves out.

30. b. In a 99 year lease the buyer does not have full ownership.

31. d. When a tenant pays fees to a landlord, the landlord must give the tenant a receipt.

32. a. In Indiana, brokers must maintain receipts of rental payments for three years.

33. c. Tenants who live in public housing may have additional protections.

34. d. Tenancy at will is a lease without a termination date.

35. d. The max fee the landlord of a mobile park can charge if he acts as the seller's agent is 10%.

36. b. The Indiana Statute of Frauds requires that all Purchase and Sale Agreements must be in writing.

37. d. Closing Cost can be found by multiplying the sales price by the closing cost percent. 378,499 x .03 = 11,355.

38. d. Indiana property managers are not required to have any type of license or degree.

39. b. According to the Lead Paint Law along with giving the new tenants a Lead Paint Notification and Tenant Certification Form, because the new tenants have a child under 6, Mike and Dana must de-lead the property.

40. a. By using the 1031 exchange, they deferred the tax on their gain until a future date.

41. c. Turn into a tenancy at will with the new owner

42. b. Qualifying ratios are calculations to determine whether a borrower can qualify for a mortgage.

43. d. Riparian rights are the rights of a landowner whose property is adjacent to a flowing waterway to use the water.

44. c. There are 3 types of tenancy for co-owners in Indiana, tenancy by the entirety, tenancy in common and joint tenancy.

45. a. The Change of Name or Request for Duplicate License form located on the Board's website under the Applications and Forms link and send in the applicable fee.

46. c. The Board will make her license inactive if she doesn't pay the renewal fee.

47. d. First time homebuyers in most states are individuals who have not owned a home in the last 2-3 years.

48. a. The Taxpayer Relief Act was enacted August 5, 1997.

49. b. Flood insurance may be required if any part of the property is in a flood zone.

50. c. The housing ratio is the front end or housing expense and the back end ratio is the total debt ratio conservative lenders tend to use more conservative ratios.

51. c. Under the Indiana Contract Law Statute of Limitations, real estate contracts must be kept for 6 years.

52. a. The formula for determining value:

Replacement or reproduction cost – accrued depreciation + land value = Value

53. d. A protected class is any group of people designated by HUD.

54. d. The Indiana Consumer Protection Law (Chapter 93A) prohibits unfair and deceptive trade practices.

55. b. The mortgage deed pledges the property as collateral.

56. c. Real Property is real estate plus bundle of legal rights.

57. a. Personal property is moveable.

58. d. Illegal purposes uses are not included in the "bundle of rights"

59. b. The economic characteristics of Real Estate are relative scarcity, improvements, permanence of investment and area preference.

60. c. Subjective value is affected by the relative worth an individual places on a specific item.

61. d. The Board can, upon application, issue a temporary license without examination to the broker's designated individual or legal representative.

62. a. A broker acting on behalf of an out of state developer must notify the Board within 7 days of accepting the client.

63. c. The seller can offer to carry back a 2nd mortgage.

64. b. Estate in severalty is sole ownership.

65. d. When a landowner's property borders a large non-flowing body of water such as an ocean, the landowner has the right to enjoy the water.

66. b. A township is divided into 36 sections.

67. a. Abbreviation for Latin term *ET uxor* meaning wife.

68. d. A chain of title is a recorded history of conveyances on a particular property.

69. c. A chattel mortgage is used with personal or moveable property.

70. b. Clustering is when a developer groups home sites on a smaller lot and leaves the remaining land for use as common areas.

71. d. A home equity conversion mortgage is another name for a reverse mortgage. This type of mortgage allows an elderly person to remain in their home in which the equity is converted to cash for the homeowner.

72. a. The Torrens System is a system of registering title to land with a public authority.

73. c. The ceiling fan became real property once it got attached to the ceiling.

74. b. Most lenders require 3-6 months of reserves of the PITI payment when purchasing income property which often creates a barrier to entry.

75. a. A license is not required when an individual sells his business.

76. d. American with Disabilities Act.

77. c. A broker cannot offer benefits to his/her independent contractors.

78. b. $325,000 - $268,901.06 = $56,098.04

79. d. Only first time homebuyers can withdraw penalty-free up to $10,000 from their IRA.

80. a. The tax credit was worth 10% of the purchase price.

81. c. No two pieces of land are ever exactly alike.

82. d. All are uses of real property.

83. c. California

84. b. The oven was a trade fixture and because he returned the walls and the floors to their original condition it can be considered personal property.

85. a. The Home Mortgage Disclosure Act (HMDA) requires mortgage lenders to collect and report data to assist in identifying possible discriminatory lending practices.

86. c. Blockbusting is the illegal act of convincing homeowners to sell their properties by suggesting that a protected class is moving into the neighborhood.

87. d. The Equal Credit Opportunity Act prohibits lenders from discriminating against credit applicants on the basis of race, color, religion, national origin, sex, marital status, age or dependence on public assistance.

88. a. The License Law was not enacted to raise revenue.

89. c. The 4 government powers are PETE: Police Power, Eminent Domain, Taxation, and Escheat

90. b. This is a determinable fee estate in which the estate will come to an end immediately if the specified purpose ceases.

91. b. All earnest deposits must be held in the company's escrow account.

92. d. Deed restrictions can control from what can be parked in a driveway to what exterior color the homes can be.

93. c. When the proceeds of the foreclosure sale do not cover what is owed, the lender may claim other assets to cure the indebtedness.

94. a. A fiduciary relationship requires that an agent exhibit trust, honesty and good business judgment when working on behalf of the principal.

95. a. He does not have to supply his tax returns.

96. b. Each partner will have to sign since they all hold title.

97. c. The fence is an encroachment because it invades the neighbor's land.

98. d. Once the grandfather conveys the property to her it is separate property.

99. b. Because a corporation is a legal entity, corporate real estate ownership is held as tenancy in severalty.

100. c. The down payment is 100-90= 10% . 10% of 318,000 = 31,800 or 32,000.

Real Estate Sales Exam III

1. What is the transfer tax the seller will pay in Indiana if he sells his home for $428,000?

a) $0

b) $4820

c) $1284.33

d) $1000

2. The contiuing education hours were waived for Wendy because she is _____.

a) doctor

b) licensed salesperson

c) broker

d) in the armed forces

3. Indiana has reciprocity agreements with _____ states.

a) 14

b) 23

c) 13

d) 10

4. Indiana exempts 4 groups from paying property tax. They are

a) disabled, blind, veterans and elderly

b) surviving spouse and children, elderly, blind, veterans

c) surviving spouse and children, disabled, elderly, veterans

d) elderly, disabled, blind surviving spouse and children

5. Arthur, the owner of 3 two family homes, decides to enlist the help of a property management company to aid him in managing the properties. What type of contract will he have with the property manager?

a) a multiple listing agreement

b) a rental agreement

c) a management agreement

d) a multiple use agreement

6. The Federal Reserve Board's Regulation B implements _____.

a) Equal Credit Opportunity Act

b) Truth in Lending

c) RESPA

d) Home Mortgage Disclosure Act

7. The Hemsley family bought a vacation home in Indianapolis. Their down payment was 40% and they financed the rest. They became the

a) mortgagee

b) borrower

c) mortgagor

d) lienor

8. Karen, who purchased her apartment in the city for $598,000, tells her friend Samantha that her property tax payment is included in her monthly maintenance fee. Samantha suspects that Karen more than likely purchased a

a) leasehold

b) PUD

c) condo

d) co op

9. The Stemmons family owns 2 thousand acres of land with several trees on the property. Every year they sell the lumber to a timber company. The cut trees are sold as

a) real property

b) personal property

c) not considered property since they are not a structure

d) an appurtenance

10. Marla, a vendee, has an equitable interest in the property located on 926 Elm Street, Any Town, Any State 12345. In this case Marla is the

a) seller

b) grantor

c) purchaser

d) grantee

11. Your home has a fence that was installed around 15 years ago and you have lived there for 12 years. You have continuously used your side of the property for 6 years without any problems. Recently your neighbor had his land surveyed and it appears as though your fence is on his land. In IN, if you continue to use the land and your neighbor doesn't say anything, how many years do you have before you can file for adverse possession.

a) 14

b) 1

c) 8

d) 20

12. An option to purchase a home for $325,000 with 120 days was sold to Heather for $9,000. After 60 days the seller accepted an offer from Heather to purchase the home of $305,000. Which is true?
a) Heather violated the agreement
b) Heather loses her option deposit
c) Both Heather and the seller are in violation of contract law.
d) Heather could make a new offer for $305,000

13. A property is worth $214,000 and it has $156,000 in liens tied to it. This difference is known as

a) the assessed value

b) down payment

c) equity

d) leverage

14. Martha and her daughter made an offer on another home based on their current home selling by a certain date. What type of clause was this?

a) financing

b) contingency

c) recession

d) partial performance

15. An agent meets with a client in their home for the 1st time and the couple decides to sign the listing agreement authorizing the broker as their listing agent. The agent loves the home and believes it would make a great starter home for Jack, her neighbor's son. The agent holds an open house and receives 2 offers along with Jack's offer. These offers are all very similar. Then just before she (agent) leaves to present the offers, she gets a new offer which is much better than the current offers. Even though she really wants Jack to get the home, she shows all offers to her client. Which of the 6 agent responsibilities did the agent demonstrate?

a) loyalty

b) accounting

c) reasonable care

d) confidentiality

16. _____ is when the municipality takes action against a property owner and through the court land process attempts to gain ownership of the property.

a) foreclosure

b) eminent domain

c) taking

d) constructive notice

17. Which is true?

a) FHA is hazard insurance

b) FHA guarantees that the borrower will not default on the loan

c) FHA 203(k) loans are for 1 – 4 investment properties only

d) FHA insures the lender against borrower default

18. Which contract is voidable?

a) a painter is contracted to paint a home, but 2 days before he was to begin the job, the home was destroyed by a hurricane.

b) an owner who grows marijuana in his backyard, agrees to sell it to his next door neighbor

c) an older brother who lives with his younger brother because he is mentally challenged and needs supervised care contracts a landscaping company to begin cutting the yard

d) a buyer makes an offer to purchase and includes a financing contingency

19. According to Indiana law, borrowers have no _____ rights after a valid foreclosure.

a) littoral

b) air

c) redemption

d) mortgage

20. Victor has a section 3 homestead and files his Declaration of Homestead with the Registry of Deeds. How much protection should he expect?

a) $100,000

b) $500,000

c) $110,000

d) $125,000

21. Another name for the government survey method is _____.

a) the rectangular survey system

b) principal surveys

c) base lines survey method

d) principal meridians

22. The Jackson Estate is sold to satisfy a judgment resulting from an $18,000 mechanics lien for work that began on September 15, 2012, subject to a first mortgage lien of $ $310,000 recorded November 17, 2011, and to this year's outstanding property taxes of $14,000. If the Estate is sold at the foreclosure sale for $350,000, in what order will the proceeds of the sale be distributed:

a) $310,000 mortgage lien; $18,000 mechanics lien; $14,000 property taxes; $8,000 to the foreclosed landowner

b) $18,000 mechanics lien; $310,000 mortgage lien; $8,000 foreclosed landowner; $14,000 property taxes

c) $14,000 property taxes; $8,000 foreclosed landowner; $310,000 mortgage lien; $18,000 mechanics lien

d) $14,000 property taxes; $18,000 mechanics lien; $310,000 mortgage lien; $ 8,000 foreclosed landowner

23. Which is subject to property taxes?

a) Non-profit hospital

b) 100 unit apt complex

c) church

d) golf course operated by the city's parks

24. Kiley, a realtor and interior designer is, more than likely a member of these two associations.

a) NRA and AID

b) NAR and ASID

c) NAR and MAR

d) REA and NRA

25. Public employees use a mill to calculate

a) hazard insurance premiums

b) mortgage interest

c) trash and sewage rates

d) property tax rates

26. Julie owns 5 acres of land that she wanted to sell to Kelvin for $800,000. But before she could sell the land to Kelvin she had to first offer it to Angelica, a holder of the right to purchase the land who decided to exercise her right and follow through with the purchase. What right did Angelica exercise?

a) bundle of rights

b) redemption

c) right of first refusal

d) contingency

27. A developer agrees to purchase 50 acres of land from the owner $600,000. The owner has agreed to carry back 20%. If the developer takes out a construction loan with a 1st - lien position, the landowner will have to agree to a _____ agreement.

a) subordination

b) percentage lease

c) conformity

d) deferred transfer

28. A listing agreement is a(n)

a) future delivery purchase

b) interest in severalty

c) estimated amount for which a party should exchange hands

d) contract between a broker and seller

29. Deprecation is accounted for in which approach

a) market value

b) cost

c) comparative market analysis

d) rent history

30. Although Jesse works as an independent contractor under his broker, the broker is still responsible for all of the following EXCEPT

a) providing a contract which clearly stipulates that Jesse is responsible for paying quarterly federal income tax payments

b) the ethical and legal behavior of Jesee

c) payment of licensing and professional fees

d) provide an agreement which defines compensation amounts

31. Windstorm insurance is mandated by

a) federal government

b) state

c) city

d) county

32. The minimum credit score set by FHA is

a) 530

b) 530

c) 620

d) FHA has no minimum credit score

33. A hearing panel found that Mary was in violation of the National Association of Realtors Code of Ethics, in addition to receiving a penalty up to $5,000 what course may she be asked to take?

a) ethics

b) Principle of Real Estate

c) accounting

d) consumer information

34. Which is an example of steering?

a) a lender only offers balloon loans to a certain group of buyers

b) a realtor tells his clients to sell his home because one of the neighbors rented his house to a section 8 tenant

c) an owner decides not to rent his home to a disabled veteran

d) a sales agent begins showing homes to more African Americans in an affluent area because she feels the neighborhood needs to be more integrated

35. Every year Jim and Opal receive an annual allotment of 300 vacation points through their timeshare program. This type of timeshare program is known as

a) rotation club

b) vacation owner points plan

c) vacation club

d) vacation ownership interest club

36. The following legal description is known as a _____.

Lots 3, 4 and 5 in Block 6 of G. Smith's Subdivision, City of Valdosta, Hampshire County, Indiana.

a) metes and bounds

b) subdivision plat

c) township squares

d) survey system

37. Margaret receives a letter from her homeowner association that she needs to replace her roof and garage door. She is very upset because she thought these items were covered by the homeowner's association since her unit is attached to other units. What type of unit does Margaret more than likely own?

a) single family residence

b) cooperative

c) townhome

d) condo

38. In Indiana the following 2 statements: *"The responsibility of the attorney for the mortgagee is to protect the interest of the mortgagee"* and *"Mortgagors may, at their own expense, engage an attorney of their selection to represent their interests in the transaction"* , must be present on the _____.

a) purchase and agreement

b) mortgage application

c) contract offer

d) deed

39. A real estate broker refers his client to US Home Warranty Company and in return they send the broker a $125 referral fee. This is a violation of

a) the Comprehensive Environmental Response, Compensation, and Liability Act

b) the Real Estate Settlement Procedures Act

c) Truth in Lending

d) HUD-1

40. First time homebuyers Kathy and Tim are purchasing a cozy home in the city of Atlanta, that they know they will only live in for 5 years. Because their credit score is 620, their lender has advised them to pay off a few credit items to raise their score, but they are very anxious and desire to be in the home right after their wedding. The lender tells the couple they are open to a subprime adjustable rate loan. In order to proceed with the loan, they must receive a certificate of completion from an approved housing counselor and _____.

a) write a letter affirmatively opting for the adjustable rate loan

b) certify under oath that they will make all payments in a timely manner

c) take and pass a loan test

d) get approval from the seller that they will allow them to purchase the home with this loan product

41. In a condominium development, which would be considered a "limited" common element?

a) pool

b) elevator

c) parking slots assigned to occupants

d) limited access gates

42. A signed standard form offer to purchase is a binding and enforceable contract to sell real estate under

a) Indiana case law

b) Indiana general law

c) Indiana county laws

43. One of the most important deadlines in the contract documents is the

a) home inspection

b) option period

c) loan commitment

d) none of the above

44. An HO-6 policy is an insurance policy for a(n)

a) PUD

b) SFR

c) mobile home

d) condo

d) Indiana judicial law

45. Maintaining upkeep and insurance on the property until closing, obtaining a smoke and carbon monoxide certificate at closing and obtaining certificate 6(d) if the sale is a condominium are _____ responsibilities laid out in the purchase and sale agreement.

a) seller's

b) broker's

c) buyer's agent's

d) buyer's

46. An appraiser will use the _____ approach to reconcile the values of a 3 family rental home.

a) reproduction

b) income

c) cost

d) sales comparison

47. Jane bought her home for $279,000 and now it's worth $333,000. It has _____ in value.

a) appreciated

b) regressed

c) vested

d) diverged

48. Sally received a letter that her home loan with ABC lending was being transferred to Community Bank. This is known as a(n)

a) takeover

b) assumption

c) assignment

d) aggression

49. When a borrower signs a security agreement where he is promising to pay, he is signing a

a) deed of trust

b) promissory note

c) bill of sale

d) offer contract

50. A disadvantage of a bridge loan is:

a) the buyer does not have to sell their current home before they purchase their next home

b) the lender might not require the buyer to make monthly payments

c) the buyer can immediately put their home on the market

d) buyers may be prequalified base on 2 mortgages and they might not meet this requirement

51. Henry's title report suggests that the property he's purchasing is free of legal issues and liens, therefore the property has a(n) _____ title.

a) clear

b) cloudy

c) good

d) efficient

52. In a home loan, which is the collateral?

a) the down payment

b) the equity

c) the property

d) the borrower's liquid assets

53. The date an interest rate changes is known as the

a) payment shock

b) balloon maturity date

c) the adjustment date on an adjustable rate loan

d) none of the above

54. Lisa makes an offer on a home and gives her broker a check to let the seller know she is serious. These funds are known as

a) security deposit

b) earnest money deposit

c) option period deposit

d) down payment

55. Which best describes an easement?

a) When a tenant who is moving out of the storefront he rented takes his cupcake oven

b) A property owner whose land is adjacent to a river, swims and fishes in the river

c) A neighbor who accesses his barn by legally crossing part of his neighbor's land

d) The state legally takes back private land to widen the highway

56. A subdivision is

a) a neighborhood in a community revitalized area

b) a housing development where tracts of land are turned into individual lots

c) when houses in a neighborhood are the same style and color

d) a neighborhood with a homeowners association board

57. A homebuyer who had limited liquid funds, obtained her home through a non - profit organization, where she helped build her home with her own labor and services. What type of contribution did she make?

a) sweat equity

b) equity deposit

c) money

d) labor

58. Ben, who recently lost his job, is considering transferring ownership of his home back to his lender as he is having great difficulty making the payments and has been unable to sell it. This is known as

a) foreclosure

b) deed-in-lieu

c) short sale

d) adverse possession

59. Stephanie and Max, first time homebuyers in the state are currently living on Stephanie's income as a teacher; but Max will be done with residency in 2 more years so they know their income will increase dramatically. In light of this, their loan officer has advised them that they could qualify for a little more house if they took out a loan that increased by no more than 7.5% per year over the next 5 years. What type of loan are they being offered?

a) four-step mortgage

b) fixed rate

c) 2-1 buy down

d) graduated payment

60. According to their lender, a couple must contribute $71,700 in the form of a cashier's check toward the purchase of the $478,000 home they would like to purchase. This amount is known as the

a) earnest money deposit

b) junior mortgage

c) down payment

d) contingency fee

61. For government loans, which statement is true?

a) They are insured by FHA.

b) They are guaranteed by RHS.

c) They are guaranteed by VA.

d) All of the above.

62. Heather conveyed her interest in a property to her brother, Barry's friend, Mike's parents, Mr. and Mrs. Olsen. Who is the grantee?

a) Mike

b) Mr. and Mrs. Olsen

c) Heather

d) Barry

63. Katy and Mickey's home was completely destroyed during the hurricane storm. When they returned to check the damages, they found their basement completely flooded and everything destroyed as the water level reached up to the 2nd floor. Which insurance will more than likely cover the bulk of the damages?

a) hurricane

b) windstorm

c) flood

d) hazard

64. Which is NOT a liquid asset?

a) money in savings account

b) 401 K

c) parcel of land

d) stocks

65. A homebuyer used a mortgage broker with Finance World to get her home loan. She used the payment coupon provided to her mail her 1st payment to Finance World. Before her 2nd payment was due, she received a letter stating that her loan was being assigned to the Bank of the United States and that the investor Duchess Bank had remained the same. Which is her current lender?

a) Finance World

b) Duchess Bank

c) Bank of the United States

d) Mortgage broker

66. If Justine has power of attorney, she has been granted?

a) limited or full authority to make decisions on behalf of someone else

b) an opportunity to represent someone in court

c) entrance to law school

d) full power to make medical decisions on behalf of someone else

67. The principal is

a) that part of the mortgage payment that reduces the unpaid balance

b) the amount borrowed

c) a and b

d) b only

68. Which best describes an encroachment?

a) You legally drive across part of your neighbor's property to access your property.

b) You continuously use your neighbor's driveway for years and he doesn't stop you.

c) You add a non legal 2nd level to your home which completely blocks your neighbors view to the sea.

d) You allow your horses to drink out of the river which is adjacent to your land.

69. Two sons are joint tenants in a property left to them by their parents. Son A has 1 child and Son B has 4 children. In the event Son B passes, who does the property go to?

a) the property is split equally between the 5 grand children

b) the property goes to Son A and his child

c) the property goes to Son B's children

d) the property goes to Son A only

70. Ansley wants to see a visual representation of when her mortgage will be paid off as well as how much money she will be paying in interest every year. This is known as a(n)

a) loan payment schedule

b) amortization schedule

c) interest rate table

d) rate sheet

71. A bi-weekly payment is one in which

a) the homeowner will make her mortgage payment every 2 weeks

b) the homeowner will make her mortgage payment every other month

c) the homeowner will make a payment 1 time every month, but on the last month of the year 2 payments will be made

d) the homeowner will make half of her mortgage payment every 2 weeks

72. Kelly is told that her ARM loan has an initial interest rate of 5.5% and that as the rate adjusts it can never go above 9%. 9% is the _____ for her loan.

a) buy down

b) APR

c) cap

d) ad valorem

73. Indiana is a _____ settlement state.

a) wet

b) dry

c) contingency

d) covenant

74. Henry sells his home to his friend Reese; then Henry gets a letter from his lender demanding full payment. The mortgage included a _____.

a) acceleration clause

b) deed restriction

c) due-on-sale clause

d) covenant of seisin

75. Murray had to go to court to get his property back from his nephew because when he granted him the property he told him that he could not sell alcohol on the premises. What type of estate was this?

a) homestead

b) ordinary with remainder or reversion

c) determinable fee estate

d) fee simple subject to a condition subsequent with right of reentry

76. Which provides the best range of property values on a particular property?

a) competitive market analysis

b) broker price opinions

c) appraisal

d) income approach

77. Jenn and Mike finally found the home of their dreams within their budget of $385,000. They had already been pre-approved for a loan based on 75% loan to value. If the sales price is $380,000 but the appraisal came in at $365,500, what is the max loan the lender will give them for this home?

a) $288,750

b) $380,000

c) $285,000

d) $274,125

78. The State of Indiana generates revenue from the sale of real estate through

a) commissions

b) transfer tax

c) down payments

d) broker and sales person licenses fees

79. Jerry, an attorney whose principal residence is in Maine, has decided to get his Indiana broker's license. What must he do to get the license?

a) take 60 classroom hours and pass the real estate exam

b) make Indiana his principal residence

c) review and follow the guidelines for Maine's reciprocity agreement with Indiana

d) pass the real estate exam only

80. Wilford transfers one of his small rental units to his son for $1.00. What will the transfer tax charge be?

a) $0

b) $1000

c) $4.45

d) $456

81. Martha pays her taxes and insurance every month inside her mortgage payment. This is known as a _____ mortgage.

a) equity

b) budget

c) escrow

d) negative amortization

82. A very famous couple chooses a city apartment near all of the amenities they enjoy so they don't have to travel too far out and risk being noticed. Their agent notifies them they did not receive approval because the condo association board believes they will disrupt the peace and quiet currently enjoyed by all the residents. Which best describes this scenario?

a) The condo association can vote in or out whoever they feel is a good match (or not) for the condo development

b) The Board is violating the Civil Rights Act of 1866

c) celebrities are a protected class and not be discriminated against

d) co ops can deny or approve the sale of shares of stock if they feel someone may jeopardize the quiet enjoyment the residents currently enjoy

83. The realtor tells a couple that because of regression, they may have to list their home at a different price than anticipated. Which best describes what is happening?

a) the neighboring homes haven't been updated and modernized as much as the subject property

b) the home has an outdated floor plan

c) the home is in disrepair

d) a school was recently built around the corner

84. When Broker Jamie takes his clients earnest money deposit and puts it in his personal account to tie him over until his next commission check comes, which fiduciary duty is he not living up to?

a) dedication

b) accounting

c) obedience

d) confidentiality

85. The Homestead Act does NOT protect you from which of the following:

a) credit cards

b) the proceeds from the sale of your home

c) a Medicaid lien from a nursing home stay

d) the proceeds from your insurance claim I f your home was damaged by fire

86. The following is which type of description commonly used in Indiana legal descriptions: North 34 degrees East 200 feet to point.

a) reference

b) bounded

c) strip

d) metes

87. Katy has a voluntary lien on her home. Which represents a voluntary lien?

a) mortgage

b) property tax

c) federal irs

d) mechanic's lien

88. Samantha's condominium unit which recently appraised at $413,000, was recently damaged in a storm. If it was currently assessed at $405,000, what is the minimum amount covered by her H0-6 policy?

a) $81,000

b) $82,600

c) $80,000

d) $84,000

89. A broker is listing a home in the state where he knows a homicide was committed. Under the Uniform Deceptive Trade Practices Act,

a) the broker has a fiduciary duty to disclose this to potential buyers

b) the broker must disclose the sequence of events related to the homicide

c) the broker cannot hold any open houses

d) the broker has no legal duty to inform buyers

90. Jane has a document which states she has legal rights of ownership for 1324 Elm St, Any Town, and Any City 45678. This document is known as

a) affidavit

b) quitclaim deed

c) title

d) trustee deed

91. Gerard has a 30 year loan where his interest rate is 5% for 5 years, then increases to 6% for the life of the loan. What type of mortgage does he have?

a) fixed rate mortgage

b) modification

c) two-step mortgage

d) fully amortized

92. The buyers purchasing Geoff's vacation home love his furnishings so much they want to buy all of it. What contract should he use in this type of sale?

a) bill of sale

b) grant deed

c) purchase and sale agreement

d) quitclaim deed

93. Mr. Jethendrux has appointed an executrix to handle his final affairs. Which person could this have been?

a) Kathryn

b) James

c) both a and b

d) neither a nor b

94. Which is the best description of a real estate agent?

a) Anyone, licensed or not, who conducts and/negotiates the sale of real estate

b) The owner and manager of a real estate firm

c) A person who sells both home warranties and property

d) A person who is licensed who conducts and negotiates the sale of real estate

95. Ricky's friend Esther is leaving the country. She has a great loan with a 3.5% interest rate and a remaining term of 20 years. Because Ricky would like to take over this loan, he sends her lender all of his income and asset documents. Ricky is trying to get a(n) _____.

a) primary mortgage

b) assumption

c) refinance

d) equity loan

96. A legal document which conveys title to a property is known as a

a) deed

b) preliminary title report

c) purchase and sale agreement

d) promissory note

97. Which is the most common type of bankruptcy?

a) chapter 13

b) chapter 7 no assets

c) chapter 13 no assets

d) chapter 7

98. Someone's credit history report is prepared by a _____.

a) mortgage broker

b) underwriter

c) credit bureau

d) notary public

99. Paula made her mortgage payment 30 days past her due date. Her mortgage is now in

a) arrears

b) default

c) foreclosure

d) bankruptcy

100. What is the age an appraiser uses to describe a property's physical condition?

a) effective age

b) longevity

c) year built

d) average age

Real Estate Sales Exam III Answers

1. a. There is no transfer tax in Indiana.

2. d. In Indiana a person who is serving in the armed forces may have his or her continuing education hours waived.

3. a. Indiana has reciprocity agreements with 14 states.

4. b. As long as they apply to the correct municipality and get approved, the blind, elderly, veterans and surviving spouses and children are exempt from property taxes.

5. c. A management agreement is between the owner of income property and the property manager which details the scope of work expected by the property manager.

6. a. The Equal Credit Opportunity Act protects against discrimination in lending.

7. c. They are doing the mortgaging, so they are the mortgagor.

8. d. Co ops are transferred as shares of stock in which there is no recording and because of this, individual property taxes are not created for the unit, but rather the Co op or corporation pays a property tax bill for the development and passes along each member's portion to be paid through their monthly maintenance fee.

9. b. The cut trees are moveable so they are personal property.

10. c. A vendee is also known as the purchaser.

11. a. In order to file for adverse possession, you must prove you have continuously used the property for 20 years, without any warning from the owner.

12. d. Both parties are free to renegotiate.

13. c. Equity is the difference between the value and the liens.

14. b. A contingency clause is when a certain act must be accomplished within a given amount of time.

15. a. Of the 6 agent responsibilities, obedience, loyalty, disclosure, confidentiality, accounting and loyalty, the agent showed loyalty to her clients by putting their interest above her own.

16. c. "Taking" is when the municipality takes action against a property owner and through the court land process attempts to gain ownership of the property.

17. d. FHA insures the lender against borrower default.

18. a. With a voidable contract the law gives 1 party an option whether or not to proceed with the agreement.

19. c. MGL chapter 244, Sec 14 states that borrowers have no redemption rights after valid foreclosure.

20. b. Because he has a section 3 homestead and he filed it with the Registry of Deeds he can get $500,000.

21. a. The rectangular survey system.

22. d. In MA order of payment is municipal lien, federal tax lien, state tax lien, condo fees up to 6 months, mechanics lien, and all other liens on order of recording, seller.

23. b. Non-profits are exempt from paying property.

24. b. Realtors are member of the National Association of Realtors and many interior designers are members of the American Society of Interior Designers.

25. d. One mill is equal to one tenth of one penny or one 1/1000 of a dollar and are often used when expressing property tax rates.

26. c. In a right of first refusal the owner gives the holder of the right an opportunity to enter into a transaction with the owner before the owner can enter into a transaction with a 3rd party.

27. a. Subordination agreements change the priority of a mortgage or lien.

28. d. Listing agreement is known as a contract between a broker and seller.

29. b. Depreciation is estimated in the cost approach.

30. c. The contract must stipulate that the agent is responsible for paying their own licensing and professional fees.

31. c. Windstorm insurance is governed by the state.

32. b. The minimum credit score set by FHA in 2010 is 530.

33. a. She may be asked to take an ethics course through the association.

34. d. Steering is the illegal practice of directing potential homebuyers away from or to particular areas.

35. c. Vacation clubs are newer timeshare programs which give members an annual allotment of points.

36. b. The subdivision plat method uses descriptions of lots and block numbers.

37. c. With a townhome purchase, the buyer purchases the individual unit and the ground below it. In addition each unit generally has its own roof and home amenities like garages.

38. b. The wording must appear on the mortgage per MGL chapter 184 section 17 B.

39. b. RESPA prohibits kickbacks.

40. a. According to MGL chapter 184 section 17 B ½ a loan officer can only make a subprime loan to a first time homebuyer if they positively affirm that they want this type of loan and take an approved class with a housing counselor.

41. c. Parking spaces assigned to occupants are "limited" to that occupant.

42. a. Under Indiana case law a signed standard form offer to purchase is a binding and enforceable contract to sell real estate even if the offer is subject to a purchase and sale agreement.

43. c. The loan commitment deadline is one of the most important deadlines.

44. d. An HO-6 policy, much like a hazard insurance policy for a home, is now required for condominiums by FNMA and FHA.

45. a. The purchase and sales agreements lays out the following seller responsibilities: maintaining upkeep and insurance on the property until closing, obtaining a smoke and carbon monoxide certificate at closing, paying the broker's commission and obtaining certificate 6(d).

46. b. The income approach is used to estimate the value of income producing properties.

47. a. When a home appreciates, it increases in value.

48. c. Assignment is when mortgage ownership is transferred from one company to another.

49. b. A note is a promise to pay.

50. d. Often times bridge loan lenders will prequalify buyers for 2 home loans.

51. a. Clear title is free of liens and legal questions and the legality cannot be challenged.

52. c. Because the borrower can lose the property due to non payment, the property itself is the collateral.

53. c. The adjustment date on an adjustable rate loan is the date an interest rate changes

54. b. The earnest money deposit lets the seller know the buyer is serious.

55. c. An easement is when another other than the owner has right of way legal access

56. b. Developers divide up tracts of land to create individual lots

57. a. When labor or services are provided in lieu of cash, this is known as sweat equity.

58. b. Deed-in-lieu is when the homeowner voluntarily transfers the title back to the lender in exchange for release of lien and payment.

59. d. A graduated payment mortgage is one in which the payment can increase by 7.5% per year over a period of time usually 5 years and then remains the same for the duration on the loan.

60. c. The down payment is generally made in the form of a cashier's check and is the initial amount that the buyer contributes upfront towards the total amount due.

61. d. Government loans are guaranteed by the Veterans Administration and Rural Housing and insured by FHA.

62. b. The individual(s) who receive title to a property is/are the grantee.

63. c. Because the home was damaged the excessive water level and experienced significant flooding, the flood insurance will cover the damages.

64. c. A liquid asset is that which can be easily converted to cash.

65. b. The lender is the actual financial institution that loaned the money.

66. a. Power of attorney grants an individual full or limited authority on behalf of someone else.

67. c. The principal is the amount of money borrowed along with that part of the mortgage payment that reduces the unpaid balance

68. c. An encroachment is an illegal improvement which intrudes another's property.

69. d. Joint tenancy has right of survivorship in which the survivor will now receive the deceased's portion of the property.

70. b. An amortization schedule is a table that how much principal will be applied to each mortgage payment. It also shows the yearly balance as it decreases until it reaches zero.

71. d. With a bi-weekly mortgage payment the homeowner pays half their mortgage payment every 2 weeks; which by the end of the year they will have made 13 payments.

72. c. The limit on ARM loans.

73. a. Indiana is a wet settlement state. Wet settlement is when funding occurs at closing.

74. c. A due on sale clause allows the lender to demand full repayment if the borrower sells the property that served as security for the loan.

75. d. A fee simple subject to a condition subsequent with right of reentry is where the grantor can go to court to get title back to his property if the grantee does not comply with the grantors condition of ownership.

76. a. The competitive market analysis helps the licensed agent/broker to identify a range of values in a given area.

77. d. The lender will lend based on the appraised value which is $365,500.

75% of $365,500 = $274,125.

78. b. Indiana generates revenue from the sale of real estate through transfer taxes

79. c. Indiana has reciprocity with all other US states for real estate licenses. He should look at the specific guidelines for his home state's reciprocity agreement with Indiana.

80. a. When the transfer is less than $100, the Registry of Deeds will not charge transfer tax.

81. b. A budget mortgage is when the lender pulls funds from the borrower's monthly payment and sets it aside in an escrow account in order to make yearly tax and insurance payments.

82. d. While they are bound by fair housing laws and cannot discriminate based on age, gender, ethnicity/race and religion, co ops do have more control than condo association since they transfer share of stock as opposed to real property.

83. a. In this case regression describes the fact that improvements have been made to the subject property that are much greater than the neighboring homes.

84. b. The Fiduciary duty of accounting states that the agent cannot commingle funds.

85. c. A Medicaid lien is a government lien and they are exempt.

86. d. Metes description gives both a bearing and a distance.

87. a. A voluntary lien is created by the lienee's action.

88. b. The HO-6 policy must provide for a minimum of 20% of the appraised value.

89. d. According to the Uniform Deceptive Trade Practices Act, "The fact or suspicion that real property may be or is psychologically impacted shall not be deemed to be a material fact required to be disclosed in a real estate transaction."

90. c. Title is a legal document evidencing a person's right or ownership to real property.

91. c. A two-step mortgage generally starts out at a set interest rate then increases after 5 or 7 years and a set rate for the duration of the loan.

92. a. A bill of sale is used in transferring personal property.

93. d. An executrix is a female appointed to administer a will.

94. d. A real estate agent is a licensed person who conducts and negotiates the sale of real estate.

95. b. An assumption is when a buyer assumes the sellers mortgage.

96. a. A deed is a legal document which conveys title to property.

97. b. A chapter 7 no asset is when the filer has no assets to pay the creditors.

98. c. A credit bureau is a 3rd party company which prepares a summary report of an individual's credit history.

99. b. Generally payments 30 days behind on first trust deeds are said to be in default.

100. a. The effective age is a term the appraiser uses to describe a building physical condition.

Real Estate Sales Exam IV

1. The sum of all of Mr. Slayer's personal property and real estate at the time of his death is known as his

a) probate

b) escheat

c) estate

d) will

2. Melody's dad, a cabinet maker, built her a beautiful entertainment unit that he securely attached to the wall 5 years ago. Now that she's married and they want to grow their family they have decided to move. The unit will have to remain in the home because it is a (n)

a) easement

b) trade fixture

c) appurtenance

d) fixture

3. A homeowner's insurance policy

a) is a warranty service contract that covers repair and replacement of home appliances

b) combines hazard insurance and personal liability insurance

c) is hazard insurance

d) all of the above

4. A servicer

a) loans money to purchase a home

b) collects mortgage payments from a borrower

c) conducts title searches

d) insures the loan in case of borrower default

5. A three family home in Indiana is

a) a dwelling with 1 deed and is for 3 families

b) a commercial property

c) not legal in Indiana

d) a dwelling with 3 different deeds and is for 3 families

6. Three homeowners live adjacent to a body of water, but their water use rights are based on when they first used or applied for use. This is known as

a) riparian rights

b) littoral rights

c) the doctrine of prior appropriation

d) the doctrine of adverse possession

7. A tenancy that is NOT put in place by operation of law but by the parties expressed intent is

a) tenancy at will

b) tenancy by the entirety

c) community property

d) tenancy in common

8. All are "improvements" except

a) sidewalk

b) street light

c) pizza oven

d) paved road

9. Which is NOT a physical characteristic of land?

a) scarcity

b) non-homogeneity

c) immobility

d) indestructibility

10. Over several years, the Parson's land ownership has increased by means of

a) regression

b) accretion

c) diversion

d) avulsion

11. David allows Mike to store his pickup truck in his driveway for several weeks free of charge. David gave Mike a (n) _____.

a) acknowledgement

b) tenancy right

c) license

d) easement by prescription

12. Marty receives a notice for specific performance of a real estate contract, which is asking for

a) an earnest money deposit

b) conveyance of the property

c) a new contract

d) a deficiency judgment

13. Which is NOT an acceptable means by which a contract can be terminated?

a) sellers decides to get a divorce during transaction

b) destruction of premises

c) mutual agreement of the parties to cancel

d) impossibility of performance

14. Timothy is out of town when his broker tries to inform him that she has a buyer for his home who has made a full price bid and given her (the broker) the $3,000 earnest money deposit. What does the broker have at this point?

a) implied contract

b) executed purchase and sale agreement

c) voidable contract

d) offer

15. Patricia, who fell behind on her mortgage payments, requested assistance from her lender. Her lender helped her by substituting her old mortgage with a newer one in which they lowered her interest rate and extended her term. What term best describes what happened?

a) refinancing

b) novation

c) accelerating

d) none of the above

16. Which of the following statements is TRUE of a listing contract?

a) It obligates the broker to convince the seller to convey the property to the first person to make an offer.

b) It maintains that the broker act as a non-agent with a seller

c) It is an employment contract between the broker and the principal.

d) It is an agreement that lasts indefinitely

17. Which statement represents what an exclusive –agency listing and an exclusive-right-to-sell listing have in common?

a) Both provide for only 1 broker to represent the seller

b) Both are net listings

c) With both, the seller only allows only 1 salesperson to show their property

d) With both, the seller can sell the property without paying a commission

18. Margaret's broker listed and advertised her property, to find Nathan, a ready, willing and able buyer. After reviewing the offer and sleeping on it, Margaret decided to reject the offer, telling her agent she had remorse and no longer wished to sell her home. In this case Margaret

a) will have to pay the buyers for any damages

b) must sell the property

c) owes her broker the commission

d) is within her rights to change her mind

19. Highest and best use is

a) the effective age of a property

b) results in its "highest value"

c) the most marketable value

d) the book value

20. All are significant factors in comparing property with the sales comparison approach EXCEPT:

a) original purchase price

b) financing terms

c) physical appearance and condition

d) sale date

21. PITI stands for

a) payment, insurance, taxes and investment

b) principal, insurance, tariff, interest rate

c) payment, interest rate, taxes, insurance

d) principal, interest rate, taxes and insurance

22. Samantha has a 15 year loan at 4.5% interest rate for 15 years. This is a

a) conventional fixed rate loan

b) fixed rate loan

c) variable loan

d) pay option arm loan

23. You will use which formula to calculate the gross income multiplier (GIM)

a) GIM = annual gross income/sales price

b) GIM = rate x value

c) GIM = sales price/annual gross income

d) GIM = value/rate

24. When a property is pledged for a loan without giving up possession, this is known as

a) substitution

b) acceleration

c) hypothecation

d) alienation

25. Greg is someone who has received training, education and is experienced in estimating real property value. His job title is a(n)

a) loan processor

b) mortgage banker

c) underwriter

d) appraiser

26. Another name for Homeowner Association dues is

a) community property fees

b) common area assessments

c) common law dues

d) apportionments

27. A(n) _____ is when a tenant is lawfully expelled from the property.

a) aversion

b) eviction

c) conviction

d) avulsion

28. Which is NOT a duty of a recorder?

a) a public official who maintains public real estate records

b) county clerk

c) transcribes real estate transaction

d) collects fees for documents filed

29. Hank and Cheri use a 1003 to

a) apply for a mortgage loan

b) write out a land contract

c) list a property for sale

d) make an offer on a home

30. Once the appraisal was completed, Jet's lender received a CRV or Certificate of Reasonable Value. What type of loan is he getting?

a) Fannie Mae

b) FHA

c) RHS

d) VA

31. _____ and _____ are Government Sponsored Entities.

a) FHA and VA

b) Ginnie Mae and Freddie Mac

c) Fannie Mae and Freddie Mac

d) RHS and Agricultural loans

32. According to Regulation Z Jasmine has _____ to rescind the transaction.

a) 5 days

b) 3 days

c) 4 days

d) 1 day

33. An employer sponsored tax-deferred retirement plan that homebuyers can borrower against is a

a) 401(k)

b) 203(k)

c) 403(b)

d) a and c

34. Jumbo loans refer to loans greater than _____.

a) $417,000

b) $650,000

c) $471,000

d) $617,000

35. The Fair and Accurate Credit Transactions Act of 2003 (FACTA) deals with

a) mortgage fraud

b) commingling of funds

c) prepayment penalties

d) identity theft

36. Which statement about mortgage insurance is NOT true?

a) is also known as private mortgage insurance

b) covers the lender when a homeowner defaults

c) is required when the borrower's down payment is 20% or more

d) is included in the mortgage payment

37. The Barksdale family just learned that the city is planning to build a small commuter airport near their family farm in which the home will sit below the flight path. They were hoping to sell the farm in a year but now fear that their values may be decreased due to

a) functional obsolescence

b) functional regression

c) economic obsolescence

d) economic regression

38. Last year, 17 year old Jonathan inherited 5 two family homes from his late father. Now 2 years later, Jonathan has decided to sell 1 of them. If he conveys his interest in the property to a purchaser by signing a deed, the contract will be

a) valid

b) void

c) voidable

d) invalid

39. Valid exclusive listings must include

a) an expiration date

b) a forfeiture clause

c) an automatic renewal clause

d) must allow the listing broker to appoint subagents

40. Meredith wanted Haley to know that her signature was genuine as she was signing a deed transferring ownership of her property to Haley. The declaration that Meredith made before a notary was a (n)

a) sheriff's deed

b) acknowledgment

c) promissory note

d) affidavit

41. Title to real estate can be transferred by involuntary alienation by all of the following except:

a) escheat

b) erosion

c) seisin

d) eminent domain

42. During her closing, Hillary reviewed a legal document which requires that she repay her mortgage loan during a given period of time based on a stated interest rate. This document is known as a

a) mortgage

b) deed of trust

c) lien

d) note

43. Zachary, whose home is set to close in 2 weeks, gets a call from his builder saying that his new home won't be ready for another 3 weeks. Zachary's realtor works out a deal where he can remain in the home 1 week after closing. This is known as a

a) leasehold

b) leaseback

c) lease at will

d) lease purchase

44. A trustee is

a) a fiduciary who controls property for the benefit of another person

b) always the executor of the estate

c) a trustworthy individual

d) an attorney

45. The best type of estate to inherit is

a) a leasehold estate

b) a life estate

c) a fee simple estate

d) a general estate

46. The time and date a document was recorded establish

a) chain of title

b) subrogation

c) escrow

d) priority

47. Rich sells a parcel of land to Tom. Tom quickly records the deed. If Rich tries to sell the same parcel to Kevin, which of the following statements is TRUE?

a) Tom will have to bring a quitclaim deed to court, since Rich is trying to sell the same property.

b) Kevin has been given constructive notice of the prior sale because Tom quickly recorded the deed.

c) Kevin was mailed the actual notice of the prior sale since Tom recorded the deed.

d) none of the above

48. The acquisition of real estate through the payment of money is

a) a sales transaction

b) called a truth in lending transaction

c) a purchase money transaction

d) a deed-in-lieu

49. A property sales price is a

a) debit to the buyer and a credit to the seller

b) credit to the buyer only

c) debit to the seller and credit to the buyer

d) credit to the seller only

50. Wilma collected a security deposit from each of her tenants when they signed their lease agreements. Now that she is selling her property, who should be credit the security deposits?

a) Wilma

b) buyer

c) tenants

d) lender

51. Because Jimmy has the right to control his property, he has a right to do all of the following except:

a) refuse to host a neighborhood block meeting at his home

b) turn away the meter reader from the local utility company

c) put a sign in his front yard that says "no soliciting"

d) host a family barbeque

52. Two properties A and B are separated by a private road. Landowner A owns the road but Landowner B has unrestricted access, as he needs to access the road to reach the main highway. What type of access does Landowner B have?

a) an easement by necessity

b) an encroachment

c) an easement

d) an assessment

53. Mena was so excited as she was purchasing her first home and everything, so far, has gone smoothly. The home inspection came back with minimal issues and her loan was fully approved. But 2 days before her closing date, the home caught on fire and was totally destroyed. Who will more than likely bear the loss?

a) Mena

b) the seller's lender

c) the seller

d) the buyer's lender

54. Contracts for the sale of real property, under the statute of frauds, must be

a) in writing to be enforceable

b) on purchase and sale agreement forms

c) started by a licensed agent

d) executed right away

55. The Martins enter into a sales contract with the Haggardy family in which they will pay the Haggardy family $1500 per month for their family farm. The Martins will pay all insurance premiums, property taxes, and any maintenance and repair costs, but the Haggardy's will maintain title to the property for 20 years. What type of contract do the two families have?

a) lease with option to buy

b) contract for deed

c) contract at will

d) mortgage contract

56. Harry lists his home with Broker Bill. He tells Broker Bill that as long he makes a profit of $203,000 on the sale of his home, Broker Bill can keep the difference as commission. This type of listing is known as

a) an exclusive-agency listing

b) an open listing

c) an exclusive-right-to sell listing

d) net listing

57. The original capital outlay for labor, materials, land and profit is known as

a) the market value

b) the market price

c) Mortgage value

d) cost

58. Kenny, a single man, died and left all of his real estate to his niece, 23 year old Ashley in a will. Title passes to Ashley at what point?

a) when she executes a new deed to all of the properties

b) after she pays all of the property taxes

c) immediately after Kenny's death

d) once she receives a title report that the properties are free and clear

59. How does a condominium differ from a planned unit development (PUD)?

a) a condominium usually has a pool and gym

b) in a PUD, an owner owns the building or unit they live in

c) a PUD has more units

d) all of above are true

60. A rate and term refinance

a) is also known as a no cash out refinance

b) generally covers the previous balance plus the costs associated with obtaining the new mortgage

c) puts cash in the borrowers hands

d) both a and b

61. Existing mortgages are usually bought as a "pool" on the _____.

a) primary market

b) secondary market

c) government market

d) black market

62. Liens and encumbrances shown on the title commitment, other than those listed in the contract, must be removed so that the title can be conveyed free and clear. It is the _____ responsibility to remove these.

a) seller's

b) buyer's

c) lender's

d) title company's

63. The principal amount of the buyer's new mortgage is a

a) debit to the real estate company

b) credit to the real estate company

c) credit to the buyer

d) debit to the seller

64. Jay's lender would like to ensure that he is paying a fair price for the home he is purchasing. In order to determine this, the lender will order a (n)

a) appraisal

b) broker price opinion

c) comparative market analysis

d) chain of title

65. For tax purposes, a (n) _____ *establishes* the value of a property.

a) broker

b) recorder

c) appraiser

d) assessor

66. Which tenancy automatically renews itself at each expiration?

a) tenancy at sufferance

b) tenancy for years

c) tenancy from month to month

d) tenancy at will

67. A valid lease has all of the requirements EXCEPT

a) valuable consideration

b) offer and acceptance

c) capacity to contract

d) county clerk recording

68. Money set aside for the replacement of common property in a condominium or cooperative project is called

a) replacement reserve fund

b) savings fund

c) capital improvements fund

d) contingency fund

69. Judith had to replace her boiler. This type of repair is classified as which type of maintenance?

a) construction

b) corrective

c) preventive

d) routine

70. Which does NOT affect zoning?

a) The principle of conformity enhances value.

b) The city requests that new building conform to specific types of architecture.

c) Values have remained the same because owners have the freedom to develop land as they please.

d) A new city ordinance mandates that the street floors of office building be used for delis and cafes.

71. Happy Family Realty received a lis pendens for their recent listing located at 7892 Oak Street. They now have

a) a notice of special assessment

b) a notice that legal action has been filed which could affect the property

c) a loan commitment letter

d) a home inspection report

72. New agent Barbara was so excited to close her first client that she gave her friend Nicholas $200 for referring the client to her. What Barbara did was

a) give Nicholas what is considered a kickback and is illegal under RESPA

b) legal as it's the cost of doing business

c) as long as Barbara had her attorney draw up an agreement between her and Nicholas, this was legal

d) illegal because she should have given the money to her broker

73. Which is an example of a unilateral contract?

a) a real estate sales contract

b) an agreement which states that you will provide sweat equity as your contribution in having your home built.

c) a contract between a broker and his agent

d) The sales manager says he will offer a 20% bonus if you sell $3.5 million in real estate.

74. The Gramm-Leach Bliley Act (GLBA) requires that companies give consumers privacy notices. Which jurisdiction does this fall under?

a) The Equal Credit Opportunity Act

b) Community Reinvestment Act

c) The Federal Trade Commission

d) The Sherman Anti-Trust Law

75. All are loan payment plans EXCEPT

a) 30 year fixed loan at 5.5% interest rate

b) 2-1 buy down

c) reverse mortgage

d) graduated payment mortgage

76. A primary mortgage loan is funded by

a) a mortgage banker

b) a mortgage broker

c) both a and b

d) neither a nor b

77. What should an owner of an apartment complex do if he has determined that his vacancy rate is less than 4%?

a) Nothing

b) He should lower his advertising budget

c) He should make property improvements

d) He should survey the rental market to determine whether he can raise his rents

78. Jacob and Leslie have a beautiful 2700 square foot home just outside the city, but most of the other homes are about 1800 square foot. Their home value has decreased because of what appraisal principle?

a) regression

b) assemblage

c) diminishing and increasing returns

d) contribution and conformity

79. Under FIRREA appraisers need to be licensed by the _____ in order to appraise real property valued over $1,000,000 in federally related transactions.

a) state

b) federal government

c) county

d) bank

80. The house on Elm Drive is for sale because last year someone committed suicide in the home. In Indiana, a listing broker

a) must tell the buyer

b) must tell the buyer's agent

c) must tell lender

d) Broker's do not have to disclose this information according to Indiana general laws.

81. A buyer's agent should NOT disclose which of the following to the seller?

a) the relationship between the buyer and the agent

b) agent compensation that will be paid from the broker's commission

c) that the agent may benefit from referring the parties to a subsidiary of the broker's firm

d) that the buyer is anxious to find a place to live

82. The art of weighing the findings and analyzing from 3 approaches to value is known as

a) substitution

b) reconciliation

c) assumption

d) capitalization

83. A prospective buyer is attracted to a property that has a negative cash flow. The following must be TRUE?

a) the depreciable base is large

b) there is no deferred maintenance

c) There is a substantial increase in property value

d) the new buyer will have to make a huge down payment

84. What provision can stop Cary from losing her home to foreclosure if she files for chapter 13 bankruptcy?

a) automatic stay provision

b) automatic stop provision

c) repayment provision

d) payment restructure provision

85. Lisa is frustrated with her homeowners association as they have neglected to fix the walkway where her mother fell. She should

a) stop paying her HOA dues

b) continue to pay her HOA dues because in Indiana HOA dues take precedence over all other liens

c) place the money she would normally pay for her dues in an escrow account until the repairs are made

d) fix the walkway with the money she would normally pay her HOA dues and send the HOA a bill

86. The Indiana carbon monoxide law MGL Chapter 148, Section 26F1/2 states that the _____ should install carbon monoxide detectors.

a) tenant

b) lender

c) realtor

d) landlord

87. Raymond's commitment letter which has not expired states his interest rate will be 4.75%. But now his lender tells him that he forgot to lock that rate in and his new rate will be 5.25%. Being that Raymond has met all of the lender requirements, which is true?

a) He will have to pay the new rate of 5.25%

b) the lender will be reprimanded

c) Under Indiana law the commitment letter may be a binding agreement

d) Raymond will have to pay the discount points to get the 4.75% rate

88. In some states the sellers must sign the seller's disclosure. In Indiana

a) sellers are not required to sign the disclosure

b) sellers must disclose ALL defects

c) sellers are required to sign the disclosure

d) sellers do not have to disclose a known leak

89. The Indiana Circuit Breaker Tax Credit deals with

a) electrical wiring in the home

b) property tax credits

c) personal property tax credits

d) riparian rights

90. Which situation below deals with the Spite Fence Law?

a) A neighbor puts up a 7 foot tall fence tall unattractive fence to get back at his neighbor

b) A neighbor puts up a 5 foot tall fence to keep his small dog in his yard

c) A neighbor puts up a 6 foot tall fence for privacy as he has small children who play in the back yard

d) A neighbor puts up a 5 foot tall fence on part of his neighbor's property

91. In Indiana, "an ownership that arises between a husband and wife when a single instrument transfers property to both of them and says nothing about the type of ownership" is

a) joint tenancy

b) tenancy in common

c) tenancy of sufferance

d) tenancy by the entirety

92. All are public records that may not be found through a title search EXCEPT

a) mistakes in recording legal documents

b) unpaid liens

c) forged deed

d) fraud

93. Mr. and Mrs. Banks have made their last mortgage payment as they have paid off their home loan. They are now ready to record their discharge. In Indiana, how much should they expect to pay for this?

a) $75.00

b) $125.00

c) $50.00

d) $35.00

94. Which is NOT a condition that makes a Indiana purchase offer conditional?

a) home inspection

b) financing contingency

c) earnest money deposit

d) review of the purchase and sale agreement by an attorney

95. Ownership of a property by one person is known as

a) remainder interest

b) entirety

c) severalty

d) reversionary interest

96. The words of conveyance in a deed are in the

a) purchase clause

b) selling clause

c) granting clause

d) heading

97. Which of the following property will have the highest capitalization rate?

a) a modernized school

b) an SFR

c) a convenience store

d) a small shopping center with limited traffic access

98. Open listings are also known as

a) multiple listings

b) nonexclusive agreements

c) exclusive rights to sell

d) net listings

99. Gilbert defaulted on his loan and the lender foreclosed. Which clause requires the lender to look only to the property for satisfaction of debt?

a) exculpatory clause

b) deficiency judgment

c) acceleration clause

d) defeasance clause

100. Grantees are protected by express covenants found in

a) bill of sale deed

b) quit claim deed

c) general warranty deed

d) sheriff's deed

Real Estate Sales Exam IV Answers

1. c. The sum total of an individual's personal and real property at the time of death.

2. d. A fixture is personal property that is attached to the real property.

3. b. A homeowner's insurance policy combines hazard insurance and personal liability insurance

4. b. A servicer collects mortgage payments from a borrower.

5. a. A three family home is a dwelling for 3 families and ownership is evidence by 1 deed.

6. c. The doctrine of prior appropriation is generally in areas of water scarcity. Water rights are assigned priority based on when the right was either first used or applied for.

7. b. Tenancy by entirety is a tenancy a husband and wife can choose that is typically not recognized in community property states.

8. c. A trade fixture is an installed item that the tenant can take with them when they end their lease.

9. a. Scarcity is an economic characteristic of land.

10. b. Accretion is the addition of land when sand or soil is naturally deposited from rivers, streams or lakes.

11. c. Permission was granted for a specified period of time.

12. b. A suit for specific performance, often times, is when there is a defaulting party. In this case non defaulting party is suing to force the defaulting party to carry out the terms of the contract.

13. a. Reasons to discharge a contract include: operation of law, impossibility of performance, mutual agreement of the parties to cancel, substantial performance, partial performance.

14. d. At this point the broker has a signed offer to present to the seller.

15. b. Novation is where the lender substitutes a new obligation for an old one.

16. c. A listing is an employment contract in which the broker provides professional services to the client.

17. a. Both the exclusive-agency and the exclusive-right to-sell listings have only 1 broker.

18. c. Since the broker performed his duties she owes him/her their commission.

19. b. Highest and best value is the most probably use to which a property is used or suited that results in its "highest value"

20. a. Original purchase price is not compared when using the sales comparison approach.

21. d. PITI stands for principal, interest rate, taxes and insurance

22. b. In a fixed rate loan the interest rate stays the same for the duration of the loan.

23. a. Gross Income Multiplier = annual gross income/ sales price

24. c. When a property is pledged for a loan without giving up possession this is known as hypothecation.

25. d. An appraiser is an individual who is qualified by training, education and experience to estimate value.

26. b. Common area assessments are also known as homeowner association dues.

27. b. Eviction is when a tenant is legally expelled from the property.

28. c. A recorder is a county clerk, who collects fees for documents filed as well as maintains public real property records.

29. a. A 1003 is the loan application form that be used by lenders.

30. d. In a VA loan transaction, once the appraisal is done the VA issues a Certificate of Reasonable Value.

31. c. Fannie Mae and Freddie Mac are government sponsored entities' that were chartered by Congress.

32. b. Regulation Z gives most borrowers 3 days to rescind the transaction.

33. d. 403(b) and 401(k) are employer-sponsored investment plans.

34. a. Conventional loan amounts below $471,000 are conforming.

35. d. FACTA was designed to enhance the accuracy of borrower financial information, fight identity theft, and expand consumer access to credit.

36. c. Mortgage insurance is required the LTV is greater than 80%

37. c. Economic obsolescence is when a property loses value due to surrounding factors such as environmental and social forces.

38. a. The conveyance will be valid as his age at the time of conveyance will be 19.

39. a. Listing agreements must have a "from and to" date.

40. b. An acknowledgment is a formal declaration before a public official such as a notary public.

41. c. Involuntary alienation transfers are generally carried out by operation of law.

42. d. A note is a legal document requiring a borrower to repay a mortgage loan during a specified period of time at a stated interest rate.

43. b. A leaseback is where a seller conveys the property to a buyer and the seller leases the property back from the buyer.

44. a. A trustee is a fiduciary who controls property for the benefit of another person.

45. c. A fee simple is an unconditional unlimited estate of inheritance.

46. d. Time and date establish of recording establish priority.

47. b. Constructive notice is based on the legal presumption that an individual may obtain information by diligent inquiry.

48. c. A purchase money transaction is the acquisition of real estate.

49. a. Property sales price results in a credit to the seller and a debit to the buyer.

50. b. The buyer should receive the security deposit credit once the deed is transferred to them.

51. b. Utility company i.e. those companies which own the equipment are generally granted an easement as they have a right to enter and work on the property.

52. a. An easement by necessity is an easement granted by law and court action that is necessary for full enjoyment of the land.

53. c. The Indiana purchase and sale agreement states that the seller must maintain insurance on the home. The purchaser can terminate the contract or they can accept the damaged property and an assignment of the proceeds from the insurance company.

54. a. The law goes back to the English common law and can be found in MGL chapter 259, section 1.

55. b. Contract for deed, also known as a land contract, is where the buyer pays installment to the seller for a specified period of time, but the seller maintains title to the property.

56. d. A net listing is based on the net price the seller will receive if the property is sold.

57. d. Cost is the original capital outlay for labor, land, profit and materials.

58. c. A will takes effect after the death of the decedent.

59. b. In a condominium the owner owns the airspace in their unit

60. c. A cash out refinance puts funds into the hands of the borrower.

61. b. The secondary market is where "pools" of existing mortgages are bought and sold.

62. a. The seller must pay off and/or remove any liens before the title can be delivered free and clear.

63. c. The principal amount is the buyer's credit as this is what will be used to purchase the property.

64. a. The lender will order an appraisal which will be done by an appraiser, someone who has been trained and educated and is experienced in estimating value.

65. d. A public official who establishes the value for tax purposes is an assessor.

66. c. Month to month tenancy renews itself at each expiration.

67. d. A lease does not need to be recorded.

68. a. Money set aside for the replacement of common property in a condominium or cooperative project is called a replacement reserve fund.

69. b. Corrective maintenance involves the actual repair of the building's equipment.

70. c. Zoning is a tool for implementing a local plan to prevent incompatible land uses.

71. b. A lis pendens is a legal notice that a legal suit has been filed which could affect the property.

72. a. Per RESPA, kickbacks are illegal.

73. d. A unilateral contract is when a promise is exchanged for performance.

74. c. The GLBA falls under the jurisdiction of the Federal Trade Commission.

75. a. A fixed rate loan is structured for the repayment of borrowed funds.

76. a. A mortgage banker is a firm that can originate, sell and service mortgage loans.

77. d. A vacancy rate lower than 5% generally indicates that rents are too low.

78. c. Improvements can reach a point in which they no longer add value but rather diminish the returns.

79. a. Under FIRREA appraisers need to be licensed by the state in order to appraise real property valued over $1,000,000 in federally related transactions.

80. d. Under Indiana general law, brokers do not have to disclose if a suicide or homicide occur in a home.

81. d. Confidentiality is an agent responsibility.

82. b. Reconciliation is the art of weighing the findings and analyzing from 3 approaches to value.

83. c. Negative cash flow can be offset by an increase in property value.

84. a. Chapter 13 bankruptcy has an automatic stay provision.

85. b. HOA dues in Indiana take precedence over other liens and they can take the homeowner to court and even force a sale.

86. d. MGL chapter 148 section 26F1/2 states that the landlord must install and maintain carbon monoxide detectors in properties that contain fossil-fuel burning equipment.

87. c. Under Indiana law as long as the borrower has met lender requirements and the commitment letter has correct wording, it is a binding agreement.

88. a. In Indiana sellers do not have to sign the Seller's statement of property condition, but they must disclose known defects if asked.

89. b. The Indiana Circuit Breaker Tax Credit deals with property tax credits for seniors over 65 who qualify.

90. a. The Spite Fence Law says that a fence that unnecessarily exceeds 6 feet in height and is maliciously erected for the purpose of annoying the neighbors may be deemed a private nuisance.

91. d. Tenancy by the entirety is when an ownership arises between a husband and wife when a single instrument transfers property to both of them and says nothing about the type of ownership.

92. b. Unpaid liens are generally found in a title search.

93. a. In Indiana the fee to record the discharge of mortgage is currently $75.00.

94. c. The earnest money deposit is not a condition of an offer to purchase a home. It lets the seller know the buyer is serious about purchasing the home.

95. c. Severalty means that all others have been severed or cut off.

96. c. The words of conveyance can be found in the granting clause

97. d. Because traffic is limited, the shopping center will have the greatest risk and therefore the highest cap rate.

98. b. Open listings are also known as nonexclusive agreements

99. a. With an exculpatory clause in place the buyer is not responsible for the debt because it acts as a non-recourse loan.

100. c. General warranty deeds contain covenants that warrant the new owner's clear and undisturbed title.

CPSIA information can be obtained
at www.ICGtesting.com
Printed in the USA
LVHW10s0226171018
593890LV00014B/512/P